D0909513

Please return or renew !
latest date

THE

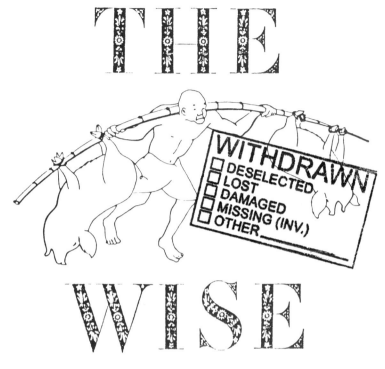

WISE

Text by Margaret MacLean

Edited by Beverley Stapells & Pam Young

Drawings by Elizabeth Stapells

TRAVEL

LER

Copyright © 1990 by Beverley Stapells

Drawings copyright © 1990 by Elizabeth Stapells

Our thanks to members of the Far Eastern Department at the Royal Ontario Museum who have read the manuscript, and in particular to the department's librarian, Jack Howard, for his many kindnesses, and also to those of our other colleagues and friends who have assisted in this work.

ISBN 0 88750 805 7 (hardcover)
ISBN 0 88750 806 5 (softcover)

Cover art by Elizabeth Stapells

Printed in Canada

PUBLISHED IN CANADA BY OBERON PRESS

For those who teach their souls to fly

Preface

The desire to learn and to know things is in our genes. Before a child can talk it is asking questions of the world through its eyes, ears, hands and feet—a process that accelerates tremendously as the child learns to speak. Why are clouds white? Where does the sky end? Why do the leaves change colour? Why won't Jane let me use her tricycle? Often the answers are ignored, but the questions flow unceasingly.

The need to know is universal among the young. This was brought home to me vividly one day in early spring in 1965, high in the mountains of Kurdistan in western Iran. Attempting to ford a rushing stream in my Landrover, I had thoroughly drowned the engine and was stuck. By the time I found a farmer with a tractor to pull us out it was far too late in the day to continue on to our destination on the Iran-Iraq border. So my travelling companion and I found ourselves spending a very pleasant evening in a large stone Kurdish teahouse. Beyond the teahouse, further up the hill, stood a village.

As we sat around the primitive iron stove keeping warm and sipping tea, the children of the village began gradually and quietly to drift into the teahouse. We may well have been the first non-Iranians they had met.

Overcoming his shyness, the boldest of the lot asked me a question. And soon the whole group was bombarding us with questions, which came at us faster than we could answer in Persian and very broken Kurdish. What is Tehran like? What is an archaeologist? Why do you come to Iran to find old things? Are there not old things in Canada? How old is Iran? Why do you carry around all these bags filled with broken bits of pottery? Have you ever been to Mecca? Do women really fight in the Israeli army? Do you have mountains in Canada? And on and on. Finally, about seven o'clock, fathers and uncles gently herded the children back to the village and class was over for the day.

By morning the river had dropped. We forded easily and continued our journey.

In reading *The Wise Traveller* you will take pleasure, as I have, in making the acquaintance of Margaret MacLean —"the Museum lady." Margaret MacLean was herself a person always asking questions. As you will see in the narrative that follows, she embarked on her Chinese adventure full of questions, and she came away with many answers. This remarkable Canadian lady was also most anxious to answer others' questions when she could—to respond to the young and their desire to understand. As the founder of the Education programme at the Royal Ontario Museum—a programme much resisted by the powers that were—she brought to her teaching the same verve and insight that characterized her Chinese adventure. For some time singlehandedly she *was* the Education Department at the Museum, and she instilled in her students not only knowledge about the collections but a sense of excitement and wonder over "the arts of man through all the ages." The Education Department at the ROM today, which now has some twenty people on staff, continues to strive for the excellence that Margaret sought in her teaching, and is in many ways her direct legacy to the people of Ontario and Canada.

The Wise Traveller is a fitting tribute to her and, indirectly, to those many teachers who, with their talents and energies, today so richly contribute to the Museum's mission by doing their best to answer questions.

T. Cuyler Young, Jr.
Director ROM

Introduction

Margaret MacLean's short book on her trip to China first came to my attention while I was writing an article about her later life, that period from 1919-1923 when she worked at the Royal Ontario Museum. The article described MacLean's many contributions to the new museum. She gave the first public lectures there and the first classes for children; not only did she teach, but she wrote articles for the press, making headlines for the museum in local newspapers. In a world of male-dominated academics, this tiny red-headed woman with a limited formal education had begun the job of making the museum accessible to the public.

Among her notes and scrapbooks was a poorly bound book, its pages beginning to yellow. It had the somewhat misleading title *Chinese Ladies at Home,* and told in vivid detail of a four-week trip she had taken in 1905 to China. MacLean had been living in Japan at the time, and the book was published in 1906 "for the author" by the Methodist Publishing Company in Tokyo. This is the book that has evolved into *The Wise Traveller.*

The travel commentaries of Margaret MacLean are noteworthy for two reasons. First, they give a colourful record of social conditions in the final years of the Manchu Dynasty, seen through the eyes of an Ontario woman. Although much has changed since MacLean was there, many of the observations and customs she describes hold true today, and as the complexity of China unfolds, MacLean's story is of value to our further understanding of that vast and troubled land. Secondly, the book reveals the mind of a bright and cultured woman from a middle-class background at the turn of the century. It is her openness of mind, her objectivity as she encounters a foreign culture and her humanity that draws the reader. For example, when MacLean talks of Chinese ceremonies for the dead in which paper money is burnt, she sees the money as "vivid tokens of faith" unlike other writers of the period who see the same activity as a "pagan rite" and a part of "idol worship." Later, in her description of the lotus and its symbolism in Buddhist thought, there is no hint of superiority or disbelief—she can see the inherent faith within the symbol, however different from those symbols to which her own Christianity had accustomed her. Likewise, she recognizes the essential religious solemnity in a "heathen" wedding. MacLean went to China to learn, not to condemn or proselytize.

MacLean pities those "intelligent foreigners" living in China who disdain the Chinese and "do not care to investigate for themselves." More often than not the foreigners that MacLean criticizes are indifferent or complacent. One writer [1] recalls that as a girl living in Shanghai, she had no Chinese friends, nor did her parents. She says:

> In some curious way it had been made clear to us that the Chinese are not quite the same as we are, that they're not exactly regular people, but *Chinese*.... Chinese are peasants out in the country...they are labourers...and servants... they are here to make life easier for us, to do all the unpleasant jobs. That's their *role*.

It was this acceptance of the status quo, this lack of understanding, that MacLean found wrong. "How ready we are to believe the 'cons' and how slow to even listen to the 'pros.'" Her abiding concern for others does not even desert her after a harrowing experience in the Shanghai riots. Narrowly escaping mishap herself, MacLean feels sympathy for one poor Chinese who was killed and "lay outside of our compound for the rest of the day."

8

It is important to remember when reading Margaret MacLean's story that it was written some 85 years ago. At that time Canadian women were for the most part homebound. Laundry was boiled in a copper boiler, cooking was done on a big coal-and-wood stove, there were no dishwashers, no vacuum cleaners. Families were large. It's true that the struggle for women's rights had begun, but those dedicated women who carried the feminist banner, who organized and persevered, were in the minority. And there were devout and courageous women who served in overseas mission fields, but they too were relatively few in number. Most women gave their time to their families, their social life centred in the church and local missionary societies. Anglicans were established, Methodists regarded with suspicion and Catholics a "papist" minority. Blacks were rarely seen and those Chinese in Ontario usually operated laundries and a few restaurants. It was a self-righteous, narrow world.

MacLean's *Wise Traveller* does more than report: she tells us what she thinks, not mincing words. Her frequently tart comments on what is happening around her do not prevent us from responding to the woman within—a woman of warmth and humour whose remarkable understanding can often surprise us. Today, in the dissolving years of the twentieth century when our concern for human rights and the success of multi-culturalism is developing, we are more careful than MacLean had to be when we speak of others, particularly in print. There are those who would even change the wording of *The Merchant of Venice* to bring it more in tune with today's thinking. Surely herein lies a danger of losing the thinking of the past. If we apply today's standards to yesterday we distort our history. We may begin to fault MacLean for using words like "peculiar" and "swarm" but we soon note that she responds to the Chinese as human beings with problems and joys not unlike our own. This was unusual thinking for the times.

In editing MacLean's book, Pam Young and I have retained the author's more "dated" observations, hoping to enable the reader to approach the thinking of a Canadian woman in 1905, as well as her picture of China in upheaval. We maintained the phrasing and flow of the original text, making changes only for clarity and comprehension. Some reorganization was necessary because MacLean seems to have written her book in daily snatches, under pressure of time, commenting as she goes. As she noted on a postcard to her father, "there is no time to write or even think."

Margaret MacLean was born in Ontario[2] in 1871, the daughter of Alexander MacLean (1834-1908) and Sarah Smith (1838-1897). She had six brothers. Her paternal grandparents were natives of Invernesshire and MacLean was proud of this Scottish blood. Her father was to become a successful businessman in Ottawa, where in 1885 he became president of the Canadian Granite Company, and later city alderman. Little is known of MacLean before 1904; nearly twenty years later she told a magazine writer[3] that at the age of ten she did not know the alphabet because she had lived "in the country" and had only five years of elementary schooling. This lack of schooling is surprising as some of her brothers attended the University of Toronto, and one was a gold medallist in classics. MacLean refers only once to her brothers in her book, when a gentleman orders her home:

A lifetime experience of brothers has taught me that such a tone is useless to resist....

and so she responds,

...meekly, in the humblest tone imaginable, as if I were a clinging creature ever dependent on the lords of creation.

During her teens MacLean seems to have spent much of her time in libraries. Later in life she claimed that everything she knew she had taught herself. Her articles for newspapers and art magazines that show an extensive knowledge of subjects that could only have come from reading. In *The Wise Traveller* she refers to the god Panku, whose beard, "like Berenice's hair was turned into stars" and in a disorderly Shanghai home she visits, her hostess is like "Mrs. Jellaby in a Chinese setting."

In 1904, her father, a staunch Liberal, was appointed by the Laurier government as Canada's commercial agent to Japan. Her mother had died, and MacLean, now 33, accompanied her father. The sprightly, organized daughter must have been a comfort to Alexander MacLean, who was 70 and quite deaf.

It was in the following year that MacLean sailed across the Yellow Sea from Japan to China. When she arrived, the country was alive with anti-foreign feeling. In the previous century Britain had begun large-scale shipments of Indian-grown opium to China, which led to the Opium Wars, and China's defeat. As a consequence, the western powers extended their trading bases, controlling the ports with imposed treaties and establishing foreign enclaves in port cities that were exempt from Chinese law. In 1900 the violent Boxer Rebellion erupted. Driven by grinding poverty, the Chinese lashed out against the "foreign devils" whose railways sliced across ancestral graves, whose missionaries had protected privileges. The xenophobic revolt was short-lived. An international brigade marched into Peking. Exacting an overwhelming indemnity, the victorious powers further embittered the Chinese with the installation of permanent foreign troops.

MacLean would have been aware of the highly charged political situation when she arrived in China, for she was an avid newspaper reader. She had also lived in Japan for a year, where her father's trade position would have exposed her to the problems facing China. But when she steps on Shanghai's Bund, "this splendid thoroughfare" with its "strange concourse of people" she is 34 years old and "out to see for ourselves" what China is really like. Her interests are less political than social: how people lived and worshipped, how they dressed. Although not a missionary herself, she had planned her trip to stay with missionary friends, in their compounds and schools, knowing that through these people she would meet the real China. When she visited Chinese homes she tended to do so in the company of mission friends and their acquaintances. Throughout her weeks of travel, MacLean senses a reciprocal warmth among the Chinese people whom she meets. It is only near the end of her journey that she experiences anti-foreign feeling and fears for her personal safety. It is then that she writes of the political situation.

> We fear the yellow peril. China fears the white peril....
> China is seething and bubbling...the people want something...they have not, but know not what it is, nor how to
> get it. They are to be pitied; so too are the officials, for they
> can see both sides—see that "young China" is too cocky
> and "old China" too fossilized...what China needs is a
> leader and history the world over shows that when the time
> is ripe, a leader will be forthcoming.

As MacLean threads her way along congested narrow streets, between rickshas and wheelbarrows, amidst coolies' calls to "make way" and peddlars shouting their wares, we can hardly help being struck by her courage in travelling alone. In Ontario, after all, for a woman to journey by herself, even for 30 kilometres, was then considered daring. In her travels generally, however, MacLean shows no concern for her safety. After touring a temple, when her way is blocked by twenty "guides" demanding money, she "straightens" herself to "my greatest height, five foot three inches" and waves the group aside. On reaching the street, MacLean's trembling companion asks, "How could you? I would have paid them all they wanted." Not Margaret MacLean.

She likes to shop. There is great pleasure in the "strangeness of the situation" as she bargains over a bronze incense burner, but discretion prevails when she avoids the shanties that display the "fag ends of everything" where "my prosaic mind dwelt more on the possibility of getting smallpox than curios," and like shoppers the world over she thinks "with regret" of the ancient coins a peddlar had offered, coins she later learned may have been several centuries old.

Though MacLean is an individualist, she is similar to her contemporaries in her attitude toward "class." She was of a generation where one's place in society was clearly defined and in China she sees the class system in action, just as in the West. When chair-bearers for a wedding refuse to work unless paid more, she snaps that "public servants of the lower orders give as much trouble as elsewhere." She finds that women of the "better class" in China are not downtrodden as she had expected them to be, but rather mistresses in their own homes. Then in a boat trip on the Grand Canal she discovers that women of the "lower classes" are "remarkable" in their own way as they guide their sampans through the water.

Class differences do not deter MacLean from sharing a wheelbarrow ride through a rural area with a local villager; nor is her inability to speak Chinese a hindrance to communication. "It is surprising how one can manage without the language of words if there be language of sign or motion, and a mutual sympathy." She and the villager have "quite an animated conversation." MacLean delightedly mimics the soaring crows and learns the Chinese word for "flying." Her companion points out coffins raised a few inches from the ground, and after she has "touched her face as if pitted"

MacLean understands that these coffins contain smallpox victims.

Even when caught in a riot in Shanghai, MacLean does not lose her composure, although later she admits that she "could have burst out crying, so great was the nervous tension." She finds it "incredible" that the people on Nanking Road who "only some fifteen minutes before appeared to be out for a holiday with no unkind word or look for me, were now ready to kill every foreigner...." Amazingly she finds a ricksha that takes her through "a cruel, cowardly mob." Reaching the missionary compound, she discovers the gate locked; guns are being fired nearby. The barrier is opened in "probably less than a minute," but, as she wryly observes, "when one is on the wrong side of a fence, a minute is a long, long time."

MacLean's skill in relating an event is enriched by her ability to capture a mood. When she climbs a pagoda "the air is fresh and sweet as it blows from the mountains...there is no sound of the countless ear-splitting noises of the city...there is a monastic silence broken only by the cawing of innumerable birds." Later she observes, "it was evening and the canal was quiet; in the boats under their hood of matting the family had gathered and here and there a flickering light...showed that the inmates had not yet gone to sleep." At a birthday celebration, "the band was playing...above was the blue of the heavens filled with stars [and then] a big moon came slowly over the great courtyard wall. What more," she asks, "could one want?"

MacLean soon recognizes the futility of being irritated with interruptions on her journey and says it is "advisable...to drift with the tide of human affairs...one may not reach one's destination quite as quickly but certainly in a pleasanter frame of mind." It is in this pleasant state of mind that MacLean ends her China trip, reflecting on the universal desire for the basics in life. It had been an invaluable experience upon which she was to draw for the rest of her life.

She rejoined her father in Japan for another two years, and then in 1908 Alexander MacLean was posted to China. He died there that December. On 18 March, 1909 the burial in Ottawa of Alexander MacLean is noted in the *Ottawa Evening Journal*. "The remains were accompanied to the city from Shanghai…by Miss Margaret MacLean." One can only imagine the ordeal the daughter faced in those three months, with her father's death, the winter ocean crossing and his final burial.

During the next six years MacLean made two round-the-world trips. Distant relatives recall the times in their childhood when their "wiry" and "talkative" Cousin "Till" came to visit, filled with stories of "bandits in Spain" and bearing gifts from the Orient. Later she settled in Toronto, near her brother John who was working for *The Globe*.

In 1915 MacLean's museum period began. For the next eight years the Royal Ontario Museum was to be the centre of her life. In her frequent visits there she had observed the lack of purpose shown by many visitors, as they moved at random among the labelled cases, with little understanding of their contents. MacLean saw the need for someone who could give life to the treasures. She applied for a position as a lecturer. Certainly she felt that her years of travel visiting the world's museums qualified her for the job. But Dr. Charles Currelly, the ROM's archaeology director, and his board thought otherwise. "There is no such position" was the terse response. They must have been surprised at the audacity of anyone considering such an undertaking without even high-school training, let alone a woman. However it was agreed that she would be allowed to do research in the building.

Undaunted, MacLean organized a programme for herself. Studying the collections and using the library, she prepared lectures on an ambitious range of topics that included, of course, Chinese and Japanese art. Many months passed and always the persevering woman was working in the museum. Years later she recalled that one day Dr. Currelly stopped beside her and reminded her that "there is absolutely no opening here for a lecturer" and hoped she hadn't misunderstood him. She hadn't, and went right on with her research.

She began writing about the museum collections for the local press. In 1915 a series of four articles appeared in the *Sunday World*.[4] She referred to Dr. Currelly, the "distinguished Egyptologist," and wrote of his care in the labelling and arranging of objects "to their greatest advantage." There was no ROM guidebook at the time and she suggests that the artifacts are "worthy of an illustrated description on the lines of Maspero's Catalog" in the Cairo Museum, adding that "in the meantime a few notes from a visitor, not in any sense an authorized version, may be of service to others...to call more attention to this wonderful treasure house."

In a subsequent article she wrote that the ROM's Egyptian bas-relief of Hatshepsut's Expedition to the Land of Punt is a plaster cast "made by Dr. Currelly" from the original in Egypt, and then goes on to emphasize the knowledge and sensitivity required for such a job. She lists books that can be read for further understanding. In the summer of 1917—still not on staff—she wrote another series on the ROM collections, this time for *Saturday Night*.[5] An art magazine of the time, *International Studio,* published a story of hers on Chinese classical painting, which was picked up by New York's *The Sun;*[6] its editor comments that "the interpretation of a Chinese Classic is interesting" and quotes the *Studio* article at length. In her scrapbook MacLean has marked this international notice with pride.

The combination of pen and patience finally brought results. About 1918 the museum board gave MacLean permission to conduct tours on a freelance basis, provided it was understood that she was not on staff. Immediately, she sent brochures to clubs and schools detailing the subjects she would teach. In her first winter she addressed some 700 people. Within the year the museum recognized her dedication—and success—and appointed her officially, to be paid $500 annually for three days a week.

She began a museum scrapbook in March, 1919 with her first tours. On the first page of the book, in her firm handwriting are the words "Margaret MacLean, Official Guide, Royal Ontario Museum." Then follows a monthly record of her teachings, listing between neatly drawn columns the subject, the group toured and the attendance. In red ink she notes what she did "on my own time." In her first month she saw 26 schools and guided more than 1200 visitors around the museum. In her summary of the first year she notes that she has lectured on 21 different subjects to 9128 people and given 31 lectures outside museum hours. She adds that she was also responsible for four magazine articles and 40 press notices about the museum. There are clippings that record teas, talks and tours where Dr. Currelly and MacLean received guests and lectured together. If their association had ever been strained, that period seemed to have passed.

"The Museum Lady," as one columnist referred to her, was an undoubted success. Newspapers acclaimed "An Official Guide for the Museum," "Woman Guide for the Museum" and "Free Lectures" at the ROM. *The Star* headlined "Woman Opens Field" and *Maclean's* ran a banner, "How Margaret MacLean Won a Niche for Herself in a Museum." The only place that failed to mention the lady was the ROM minutes, consumed with directions, authorizations, acquisitions and payment of accounts.

She was a tireless publicity agent for the museum. Typical of her enterprise was her response to hearing that a New York fashion designer had been invited to speak to the Canadian

Women Designers Association. MacLean invited the designer to the museum for a tour of the dress and textile collections on the morning before the talk was to take place. That evening, the speaker referred to the ROM "at least a dozen times...a splendid advertisement for the museum." Naturally MacLean had notified the press, and the following day there were stories—all mentioning the ROM—in Toronto's four daily newspapers. On another occasion, the editor of *The Globe's* children's page was asked to join a lecture for youngsters on Norman and Saxon times, which resulted in a glowing story about "fun" in the museum. When *The Globe's* church editor saw the clay tablets from Babylon with MacLean, he wrote of the ROM's "veritable treasure house of Biblical illustrations." At the same time MacLean continued with her own writing in *International Studio, Saturday Night* and a Canadian trade magazine, the *Canadian Jeweller.* She also visited museums in Boston and Harvard.

As a teacher MacLean gave sparkle to her facts. She liked to communicate and did it convincingly. She could "create an environment around the simplest object," recalled Dorothy Haines Hoover, the guide who was to succeed her in the museum. Hoover remembered the mediaeval world MacLean wove in the gallery when she lectured on the subject.

You could imagine the banners hanging above and almost see the rushes on the floor and hear the dogs barking...she made everything alive.

In MacLean's notes she recalls that a clergyman who often came to the ROM once told her, "You don't know how you help me [compose] my sermons." Perhaps she told him of the faith she had seen among non-Christians in China, or perhaps she gave him her view of the resurrection of the Egyptian god Osiris, "so strangely like that of Jesus Christ." If so it is no wonder the minister said to her, "Your point of view is so different!"

The Saturday Morning Club, now an integral part of the ROM's programme, was also MacLean's idea. Today most museums have special activities for young people, but in 1919 the concept was almost unknown. MacLean invited specialists in their field to talk to the group and then tour the relevant galleries. But the venture lasted less than a year. MacLean sadly records its demise when only three of the 25 club members turned out to hear a talk on decorative ironwork by a Toronto architect. "Members were so lacking in honour and loyalty to the club...when an outsider came to speak," that she decided to "disband" the group.

Two letters of importance in the museum archives give a further picture of MacLean. They are written to her by George Crofts, the museum's purchasing agent in China. She had corresponded with him, and although her letters to Crofts are lost, it is evident from Crofts' responses that their exchange was an affable and scholarly one. She discussed his various acquisitions, visitors of note to the museum and on one occasion questioned his interpretation of a painting, enclosing a sketch to make her point. In one letter he writes:

> Your letters, like yourself, are intensely interesting...they contain a mass of information clearly illustrating the great ability you possess.... I had the pleasure of listening unknown to your goodself, to two of your lectures, and was really surprised at the depth of your knowledge and the clearness of your explanations. I rather envied you the faculty and fullness of your expressions, which conveyed so much in very few words....

At the top of this letter MacLean has written, "I thanked him for the amber beads."

Not all of MacLean's relationships were so rosy. A curator told the museum directors that she had "interfered in the galleries." MacLean complained that the cold building in the winter months was "injurious to health" and was upset when the galleries were closed "without asking me," forcing her to break "engagements already made." She had taken a year's leave of absence for archaeological research, but on her return in 1921, her records show that she is tired. Her classes are large, with often more than 40 in a group, and she asks for more lecturers. There is a February evening reserved for members of the Ontario Legislature and "only three came." She has the "flu." There are ice storms. Several schools "forget to come." She has a bad foot and cannot tour the galleries as she would wish.

Abruptly at the end of 1923, she writes that she has resigned, effective the following February, due to ill health. "The Board of Trustees said many kind things about my work" and though "the Board was hard up for money at the time" she was given a present of $300, which was the "first time a present was ever given to a staff member who had resigned." She had reached page 77 and the end of her museum record.

MacLean's last years were spent in travel. In 1931 she died in a hospital for the terminally ill. She bequeathed to the museum many of her books on Japanese art, her brother's war medals, some Korean textiles and pottery and a lace christening dress. There was no mention of her death in the ROM minutes and newspaper obituaries were brief, with no reference to her eventful life. The record of her past is in her education notes, her Japanese scrapbook (in the Far Eastern Library at the ROM) and in the story of her Chinese travels.

But if her death was unremarked, MacLean's life was one of adventure. Her belief in the human spirit fuelled a quest for understanding that she unfailingly found exciting and passed on with enthusiasm. "You do give me such full moments of your life," wrote a friend. MacLean was interested in everything, and would attempt most things. In the museum she loved there were two teachers on staff by 1931, the reinstated Saturday Morning Club was drawing members and school classes were growing.

Years before, when MacLean went to Soochow, she was deeply moved when she visited a Chinese garden, so different from the Western style with its grass and flowers. This was a garden of lava and rock, where little ponds were spanned by zigzag bridges, and dishes—"broken for the purpose"—were set in patterns on paths. She felt she was in a place rich with symbolism; there was purpose and plan in the position of each stone and tile.

In the East everything of this sort has meaning…nothing is done on a hit-or-miss plan. Every detail is governed by a rule; there are rules for perspective and proportion and these are strictly adhered to…. I felt as if in the presence of a great mystery. Everywhere right at hand there was something, if only one's eyes were opened to see.

For Margaret MacLean opening her eyes and the eyes of others to the nature of that mystery was a sufficient reason for being.

BEVERLEY ECHLIN STAPELLS

[1] Elfreida Read, *A Time of Cicadas*, p. 98.
[2] Records state only that she was born in Ontario. She may have been born in Cornwall, where her father was editor of the *Freeholder* at the time.
[3] Gertrude S. Pringle, *Maclean's Magazine*, 15 May, 1923.
[4] Toronto *Sunday World*, 17 March, 1915 and successive weeks.

[5] *Saturday Night,* 24 March, 1917; 9 June, 1917; 15 September, 1917.
[6] *The Sun,* 12 August, 1917.

Chapter One

In which Margaret MacLean arrives in Shanghai, goes walking on the Bund, shows her skill at shopping and makes observations on the French Settlement, Chinese food and the eating of rats.

Can this be China?

Can this be the China that travellers have talked of? The China that filled us with pity for its inhabitants and awakened our desire to see for ourselves?

Yes it is. But it is a China Westernized and appearing as a delightful place of residence. There is the great Whang-poo River, with a park along the water and then a wide boulevard with a row of handsome buildings equal to those of any European or American city. Should one arrive on a Sunday morning, Shanghai would appear like any self-respecting Western town; church bells ringing and families going to church, the Western children looking fairer and cleaner than in their homelands. This piety is only a passing impression, though, for in the suburbs golf is being played, paper chases are being run, and Sunday is made into a day of sport. This also may be Western, but is hardly Sabbath-observing.

It must be remembered that this, my first view of China, is at its entry port Shanghai, where there is a large foreign colony. In reality, Shanghai is not, after all, far from London, England. You look surprised at this! I am thinking of two Canadians I know who stood on the Bund in Shanghai one day and in eighteen days less one hour, they were standing on the streets of London. They had crossed Russia by rail.

The Bund, the first street in Shanghai that the traveller sets foot on, is a splendid thoroughfare filled with a strange concourse of people, making it difficult to tell what country one is really in, for the buildings are mainly Occidental and the people mainly Oriental. The lower classes of both sexes in China wear garments of a hard, bright-blue colour that seems to stand out conspicuously, absolutely refusing, even when toned down with many coats of dirt, to harmonize with the surroundings; and the lower classes, the *leer-mong,* swarm everywhere.

"Swarm" is not usually the word when referring to people; but China is not an ordinary country and the Chinese swarm; no other word so fitly describes the condition. Add to these, representatives, in national costume, of almost every country in the world and a medley of ways of transportation from the burden-bearing coolie and the Chinese wheelbarrow to the Englishman's or the wealthy Chinaman's brougham with plate-glass windows, or an automobile, and then you have only a faint idea of the traffic on the Bund in Shanghai. When you see, dashing past, broughams and victorias with coachmen and footmen in correct costume and high dog-carts driven by stylish young ladies, you exclaim, "Can this be China?" You know it is, for no sooner are those words spoken than you see a dark, gloomy looking sedan chair bobbing along on the shoulders of two coolies while a third runs ahead shouting "clear the way," or the Chinese equivalent.

If the chair contains a man he can be seen fat and sleek (I never happened to see a thin Chinaman riding in a chair), and clad in silk brocade garments that in winter are fur-lined; but should the occupant be a lady then the curtain is drawn and all that can be seen are her two tiny feet always daintily clad in embroidered shoes. Old time etiquette demands that a lady should not be seen when on the street; not so with the women of the lower classes, for they pass sitting on the shelf of the wheelbarrow.

The traffic at the corner of the Bund and Nanking Road is, in fact, a veritable piece of London, in the East. There stands the English bobby, looking as if he had just come from home

24

on the last steamer, guiding the strange medley of vehicles and people, and assisted in his task by handsome Sikh policemen in the regulation uniform, save the headgear, which is a scarlet turban wound in true Indian fashion around and around the head so that the bands of silver thread that glisten in the sunshine come over the forehead; and a third set of policemen, the Chinese, whose uniform is a combination, foreign and native, but that looks neat and clean, particularly when compared with the dress of those whose way he helps to guide. The law compels all drivers to indicate, by the raising of an arm, which way they intend to turn.

Nanking Road is the fashionable drive, and in the late afternoon, it is thronged with people, both Chinese and foreign, showing off themselves and their carriages. Carriage attendants are called *Mafoo,* and no matter how many there may be, the coachman is Number one *Mafoo;* these people are the most ludicrous to be seen in Shanghai. Picture, and keep from smiling if you can, a lady dressed in the latest Parisian fashion driving in a stylish dog-cart with her *Mafoo* standing behind, dressed in a white nightshirt-looking garment upon which lies his long black queue like a spinal column and on his head, a light brown fedora. This is not an exaggeration. I saw it.

Shanghai, in general, is in a state of transition. What the foreigners disapprove of they say is Chinese; what the Chinese disapprove of is foreign. Nanking Road is a strange mixture of countries; there are large shops representing the business firms of many European and American cities, while squeezed in between these will be a native shop, open to the street, being windowless and doorless but brilliant with black or red signs, always gold lettered with the queer, fantastic hieroglyphics of the country's language. Signboards are a conspicuous part of the decoration and the characters are so large that he who runs may read if he be able.

Smells permeate everywhere and are a constant reminder that the country is China. Whether it be the subtle smell of incense or of opium (which one lady told me smelled like fried bacon), do not investigate but just classify it as Chinese for it will be with you as long as you remain in the land.

The streets in Shanghai are not all as are the Bund and Nanking Road; there are mean ones, hidden up alleys and by creeks, and can be seen by a walk along the Quai des Fosses and the Quai de la Breche that runs along the moat that surrounds the old native city. The water in this moat is filthy and at low tide is only sufficient to keep the bottom muddy, yet people wash their rice and food in it, use it for cooking; and they live. Eating only well-cooked foods has been the salvation of the Chinese, for had not instinct warned them that only by prolonged boiling would germs be killed, there would be no Chinese left to inhabit those boats that are home for so many.

I will describe this next section because it is as a fringe to Shanghai and is neither true Western nor Eastern. It is a part of the French Settlement, which the French, after naming the streets, left to grow as it would. When one goes into the French Settlement, one expects to hear French spoken and perhaps hear Chinese with a French Accent. This I did not find. The names of the streets and a few large buildings with RF in letters of gold on them are unmistakable. If you go near enough to the Bund, a "sergeant de ville," absolutely the same as is seen in Paris—peaked cap, waxed moustache, baggy red trousers, blue cloak—and beyond him, a Frenchified Chinese policeman, are all that is seen to remind one of the French municipal government. An occasional shop displays not a French sign as expected, but an English one; and many of the better class of shops have their business card printed in English, which is fast becoming *the* foreign language in China. Signs indicating that English is taught therein are seen quite often. One, in a prominent place, read:

English Language School
   Every night at seven o'clock begin to reading—
   and at nine o'clock be left.

When once the Rue de Consulat, the main street of the

French Settlement, is passed and no policeman are to be seen, and being unable to speak a word of the language of those who swarm around, one knows not what the next moment may bring forth. Each small street is devoted to one branch of business, and in every nook is either a fortune-teller, a public letter-writer or a barber at work. I saw a pedlar on the roadside with some queer looking things that I thought might be coins in a bunch or keys, some with miniature dagger hilts and some like paper knives.* Later I learned that the coins representing crude human forms were the most ancient of all Chinese coins; the paper knife-like ones were 1000 years old and had the Emperor's name writ in ancient characters on the blades; others were more modern, being only 800 and 600 years old; a few were not coins, but charms resembling money, and as amulets, they were of as much interest as the coins. Later, I picked up some coins in Soochow, but I think with regret of the ones I did not buy in Shanghai.

Along the creek-side are shanties or improvised shops, where the owners display the fag-ends of everything, hoping someone may find a use for each article. There are clever people who can pick up things valuable and rare and ancient in these shanties, but the uncertainty of finding treasures prevented me from going close to these evil-smelling places; my prosaic mind dwelt more on the possibility of getting small-pox than curios.

Shopping elsewhere in Shanghai, I quickly learned never to give the first-named price; in China, that is not expected. The price is named; the buyer objects; the seller always says, "How much you give?" Thereupon, the buyer states his price, which must be below what he is willing to give. Each knows that the other has gone to an extreme, yet such preliminaries are necessary. Finally, while the buyer is remaining firm on, say, $85, and the seller on $90, as happened to me one day, the seller will say, "You give $2.50 and I give $2.50." All right. The deal is then closed at $87.50.

Another time, finding the price of a vase to be $12.00, I offered the contents of my purse, $1.20 and a 10-cent postage stamp, but my humble offering was scornfully refused; not being discouraged and persisting, I bought it for $3.00 and the polite way I was treated made me know that either I had paid far too much, or that they respected my business ability, probably the former.

In shopping for provisions, too, you must distrust everything and everybody. At first, this is repugnant and you refuse, but when you see the natives buying from each other and find that *both seller and buyer weigh the purchase,* and know that both scales are favourable to the owners, and therefore a proper weight must be argued out; and when you see natives accepting money in change only after ringing it to test whether it be good or bad, you realize it is necessary to look sharp to one's own interests. It is impossible to be up to all the tricks of each trade. The *jinrikisha* coolie, to whom you paid a twenty-cent piece, will quick as a flash show you a bad coin and claim it is the one he just received; you know it is not but can do nothing but take it back and pay another. (Bad money is not a total loss. I had a bad dollar but received for it 85 cents.)

Cooks keep the household accounts in "cash" and as the value of a cash varies each day, they could not be honest even if they would. A cash, ordinarily speaking, is the twentieth part of a cent but tourists, or indeed foreigners in general, have nothing to do with such small money as cash unless they know the exact rate of exchange. Money exchangers are all over the city; and one day, wishing to get small change for a dollar, I received from one of these men the necessary pieces but held out my hand for more—merely making a guess that he had not given me enough—so he added a cent or two; thereupon, I held out my hand again in spite of his disclaimer and received a few cash. I do not know what would have been given had I held out my hand a third time.

It may have been my innate Scotch canniness or my few years living in Japan that made me less susceptible to the blandishments of Chinamen, and my shopping satisfactory except in one case. This was a very beautifully made rosewood chair, carved in graceful curves, and inset with a piece of marble the natural grain of which formed a picture of mountain tops with a few birds flying across. The owner of the chair could not speak English, nor yet French, although he lived in that settlement, so by a showing of money and fingers, I understood him to say $6.00, but when I offered $3.00 for it, I quickly learned it was $60.00.

At the present day, when so many civilized people are "on a diet" and when all new combinations of food advertised as pre-digested are welcomed, a few words on the food shops of China may be interesting. On the whole, shops are fairly clean and tidy, except the food ones, which are distinctly dirty. Everywhere are restaurants, open to the dust of the street, which are more like witches' kitchens, as they have great cauldrons of bubbling stews, and from the ceiling hang strange looking foods. It is just what we pictured in childhood days when listening to some fairytale. This was like the story before the good fairy came and conquered the witch. One travel book observes, "it is not every foreign stomach that can stand the sight of hundreds of greenish-brown worms, fresh from rice fields, exposed for sale."

I once asked a Chinese lady if the *leer-mong* ate rats and she claimed never to have heard of such a thing. Yet why should we make such a fuss about a poor Chinaman eating a rat? As though a rat could have a more objectionable taste than some of our cheese—Stilton or Limburger—or game that is very "high."

*"Knife" money dates from the sixth century BC to third century BC and other areas had "spade" or weight-shaped money.

Chapter Two

In which Margaret touches on the quiet conflicts within the foreign community, visits the lovely home of the Family Ku and describes the excitement of the crowded streets.

My object in going to China was to see as much as possible of Chinese life, which would have been very, very little had I stayed at a foreign hotel, or in the house of most foreigners who are not missionaries. These foreigners are ever ready to denounce the missionaries in every way, quite unconscious of the fact that they are only displaying their own gross ignorance instead of their superiority. This style of foreigner, and he is only too plentiful, is a vastly superior person; nothing in the country is good enough for him and his, yet he stays here and squeezes every cent he can out of the country while abusing it and its people. Even when he has accumulated wealth, he does not leave the constantly abused country. Why? Because he would find his social standing less high in his much-valued homeland. Ask him for information—reliable information—about the country and the answer is always the same "I don't know. We (the tone implies such immeasurable superiority) never have anything to do with them" (here again, the tone

conveys a depth that is beyond human measurement).

Most foreigners who are not missionaries speak pidjin-English to the Chinese and know almost nothing of the people in whose country they live. Each one to whom I told my interesting Chinese experiences would say, "Are there any nice Chinese?" or "Oh, how could you go into their homes? My husband will never allow me to go near them." This was accompanied by a shudder to add emphasis and also to show that contamination could be the only result. This way of speaking of the Chinese as though they were the scum of the earth was annoying, yet filled me with pity that intelligent foreigners should live years in a country and not care to investigate for themselves, and be content to take false hearsay for truth. How ready we are to believe the "cons" and how slow to even listen to the "pros."

I am not a missionary but had the much-valued privilege of staying, while in China, in the homes of missionaries, and found that they could, and gladly did, give information about the country and its inhabitants, also that they had entree of the exclusive homes of the Chinese and were welcome. So when I heard I was to call at a beautiful Chinese home near the West Gate, I was delighted.

But this emotion subsided when the *jinrikisha* stopped outside a modest brick house showing a double door and two windows, with the name "Ku" on the door. It seemed to be the home of a thrifty working man and its only beauty, perhaps, would be the contrast of quiet within to the hub-bub and filth on the street. Within minutes, though, I was to know that I was inside one of the finest homes in Shanghai, and the exterior appearance was of no moment.

The door opened and we entered the stable; sedan chairs sat like coffins on either side of the room while a horse harness hung carelessly over poles (showing that somewhere near there doubtless was a horse). My delight returned when we

passed through into a courtyard where beautiful chrysanthe-
mums were massed, and upon which the house faced.

The Ku family are not of ancient lineage, but wealthy and
progressive. The home was magnificent, but not ostentatious.
From the courtyard, one passed between great wooden
double-leaf doors. They were of exquisite design, with pearly
oyster-shell lights held in place by intricate lattice-work. The
doors opened into a large reception-hall with ceiling vaulted
and floor of stone, artificial I think, for it was so level. Tables
and chairs were arranged alternately at right angles from each
end of the place of honour where Ancestral Tablets are kept
and where incense always burns. In the orthodox Chinese
fashion, the humblest seat is farthest from the place of
honour, of course, and occupied by the hostess. Being pro-
gressive, Mr. Ku must have some modern improvements in
his home, so one of the reception rooms had floors of tile,
while another had the stone floor covered with a rug. The
length of this room was artistically broken by a beautifully
carved arch in which rested valuable ornaments.

It was late in the afternoon, and to see the garden by day-
light we had to leave the house before one half of it was seen
and go up a staircase built for the tiny feet of the Chinese

women and therefore causing us foreigners with our big feet to nearly come to grief. This staircase led to a covered passage that crossed over a narrow street and then to stairs, equally treacherous for foreigners' feet, that when we descended took us to the middle of the next block where the garden was. This beautiful home, hidden in the centre of one block and its charming garden in the centre of the next block, made one blink one's eyes and say, "Am I dreaming?"

Ah! one could easily forget the chaos of the Chinese streets; indeed one had to force oneself to remember that everywhere was not as that garden was that afternoon at sunset: the sky was a clear orange colour that shaded off into various tints, and a new moon, seeming of exceptional size and beauty, hung very low; it was one of those moons where the whole disc can be seen faintly but the patch of light circling one side was as of pure pale gold. Against this background were the curves of Chinese architecture that are so graceful and picturesque. The roof-ridges ended in the shape of a boat, and the boat had figures sitting inside, but this was a detail not at first observable. As twilight deepened, the lights within the garden house brought out the perfection of the designs of the latticed doors and windows, making a real Eastern picture.

When it was time to leave, we passed again through the stable into that horrible street; what an uproar there was! Coolies, wheelbarrow-men, ricksha-men, all screeching at each other and getting into each other's way and each man as dirty as he could be, with his queue tied up in a knot, looking like a shrew's ill-kept head. One coolie rushed by, his bamboo pole weighed down by pigs. Yes, pigs hanging upside down, squealing themselves hoarse, their legs tied firmly to the bamboo. Swarms of people shouting and jostling each other; congestion of worn-out *jinrikishas,* of wheelbarrows laden with passengers and freight, of coolies with burdens suspended from bamboo poles, of prisoners tied in a bunch by their pigtails, of

34

Chinese police with hats of bamboo-like inverted cups, of silk-arrayed gentlemen, of sedan chairs, of hobbling women, of dogs the colour of dirty white, of beggars hideous with sores and leprosy and of travelling kitchens emitting overpowering odours. And in the midst of all this bedlam stood an elegant rubber-tired brougham waiting to take us home.

Contrasts such as these are everywhere. Occidental and Oriental are side by side. Here, on one side of the road, is an up-to-date steamroller, while on the other side is a stone roller being pulled by eleven coolies while the twelfth followed and swept off the pebbles and earth that gathered on the roller, and what the thirteenth did I could not discern; there, a wheelbarrow, or a sedan chair, would be disputing the right-of-way with an automobile or a bicycle. The streets were ever a source of amusement, whether it were rain or sunshine.

One of the frequently heard sounds on the streets in China is the twang of the cotton bow as it whips the hillock of white fluffy cotton into shape for a quilt-lining. The man is always bare to the waist and the bow is fastened to his back and comes up over his head, and the string reaches down in front of him to the cotton.

As in Japan, most of the domestic work of the poor people is done on the street. They do not seem to know that Monday is the prescribed "washday," and as they have never seen an iron they cannot know that Tuesday is ironing day. (I knew a lady in Canada who could not go to a picnic one Friday because Friday was sweeping day. There are no such Fridays in China.) No matter what day one wanders along the streets, women may be seen sitting at low tables at the front doors—I do not believe there are any back doors—with a garment spread upon the table. After soaping, it is scrubbed with a brush until satisfactorily cleaned, and then it is rinsed in a tub that stands where a sidewalk should be. This is a modern city way of washing and I suppose befitting the advanced Shanghai times. Their sisters in the interior go down to one of the many canals that intersect country and city and souse the garment, then lay it out on a stone and hammer the dirt out with a long wooden stick. Often as I have seen the washing done in this way, I have never seen it at the clean stage.

Chapter Three

In which Margaret investigates religion in the foreign community, sees ghost money burnt, learns of Panku, questions the Evil Spirit and visits the Temple of 800 Gods where she shows presence of mind.

On my first Sunday in China, I went to a Chinese Sunday School from curiosity, but went again for the pleasure of watching the expressions on the faces of the teacher and students, particularly in one class where a dainty Chinese young lady was teaching street urchins. The teaching was all in Chinese and at that time, I had been less than 24 hours in the country. I was very proud of being able to figure out, from the resemblance of words to the Japanese (although the spoken languages are very different), that she was teaching the words of "Jesus loves me," but the lesson was beyond me. Fortunately, however, the Principal interpreted it for me. The teacher was telling of a little girl who was on the street when it was bitterly cold, and one of the girl pupils said, "Yes, I know what that is like, my feet have been blue with the cold," and a boy pointed to me and said, "Look at her clothes, she won't feel the cold."

Having impressed them with the misery of the world, the

teacher talked about Heaven. The attention of her ragged class was riveted on her and a little boy who was hanging on her every word breathlessly asked, "Will there be foreign candy there?" The little teacher gravely assured him that, "there would be." Now, it is not for us to sneer and say there will not be foreign candy there. Foreign candy represented all that was lovely, all that was desirable to that forlorn little piece

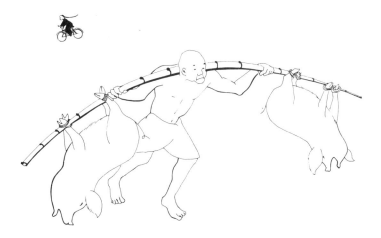

of humanity; it was his highest ideal of bliss, and to have shattered his standard might have been fatal to all further progress; besides, who knows but that the ideal we hold may be as far from the reality as his is from ours.

The Sunday School was arranged on our plan—there being no Chinese one to interfere—and it was delightful to hear these happy-faced little ones sing the familiar tunes in exactly the way our little ones do, only using Chinese words. Everyone knew the first verse and chorus and all sang heartily; most knew the second verse; few knew the third verse; only those who could read knew the other verses, but all knew the chorus and revelled in it, singing it as only children can.

In this school, no screeching was allowed so it was sweet to hear the children's voices raised in praise. Being with Chinese as I was during their hours of public worship, in church, in Sunday School and at morning devotions of the school, it brought out clearly to me the fact of God's universality. In theory, we believe that our God is everyone's God, but our practice often gives the impression that He is our God only. There, everything externally was different—the people themselves, their language, their clothes and their customs—but their needs were as ours, and they were worshipping in verity and receiving that which helps because asked for in sincerity. I was impressed as never before that God is indeed the God of the Chinese.

In Shanghai, every house, no matter how small or poor, is furnished with an altar, which oftentimes can be seen from the street, with its incense burning and its food-offering for the dead. On the walls around, hang gaily coloured vertical strips covered with strange lettering, but these do not appeal to one as much as do the offerings of drink and food, and the burning of paper money, paper clothing, paper houses, paper sedan chairs; indeed, copies in paper of everything necessary in lifetime: these are vivid tokens of their faith.

Ancestral worship is the basis of Chinese religious belief. That which a Chinaman desires, above all else, is a son to keep green his memory and attend to his wants in the next world. The spirits that pass after death into the other world have necessities, and want comforts; and so the faithful descendants of the dead have need to send them houses, boats, clothing, sedan chairs and money. It is a make-believe offering, for the luxuries bestowed upon the spirits are in the form of paper models or emblems. These paper things are burnt and their substance floats away in smoke to the grateful acceptance of the expectant dead.

On one of the busiest modern streets in Shanghai, I saw a Chinaman burning a pile of "ghost money" for the benefit of some departed one; again, on a similar street, a small table of new wood with a bowl of rice and something else on it stood on the sidewalk, while in the doorway of the house was a woman making forms of worship. This food would be, as the money, for some dear one who had died, lately or long ago, as the case might be.

Chinese history begins with the opening of heaven and earth and they have accounts of their own of the creation. The most popular being of Panku, who in art is represented with hammer and chisel, bringing the rude masses of chaotic matter into shape. His labours lasted 18,000 years and each day as the heavens rose and the earth expanded, he increased in stature six feet; at last, his task being completed and the earth made fit for its future inhabitants, he died and benefited the world as much by his death as by his life, for his head became mountains; his breath wind and clouds, his voice, thunder; his limbs were changed into the undulations of the earth's surface, his flesh into fields; his beard, like Berenice's hair, was turned into stars; his skin and hair into herbs and trees; his teeth, bones and marrow into metals, rock and precious stones; his dropping sweat increased to rain; and lastly, the insects that stuck to his body were transformed into people.

I prefer the Darwinian theory. But I can understand how naturally Chinese came to their conclusions, for insect life and people are so intimately connected in China. No need for entomologists to hunt for insects: insects are no respecters of persons and find their victims wherever they may be; they are not, like the evil spirits, easily deceived.

The evil spirit is considered a terrible creature but he can be tricked. It has always puzzled me that the evil spirit's influence could be deemed so powerful when he is so easy to outwit. For example, in China spirit-walls are built in front of doors. These are free-standing walls and placed directly before an entrance! The evil one can see, or at least know, that the door is there but can have no knowledge of the wall that protects it, for as he can only go in straight lines, he attempts to enter the door and goes bang up against the wall and shoots off down the street; again, if he tries to slide down the ridge of the roof, he is shot into the air by the end of the ridge being curved upward. It would seem as if he were a shuttlecock that must constantly be kept moving or disaster will come. A boy will wear an earring so that the evil spirit will think he is a girl and not worth venting his evil influence upon. At a certain time, New Year's I think, the evil spirit can get beyond the spirit-wall to the very door of the house but there hangs a mirror in which he sees his ugly self and thinking it another evil spirit, he hurries away. Firecrackers and noise will also frighten him, and as noise is cheap, it is plentifully used.

Judging from the population of the country, the temples are not much frequented by worshippers—notice I say worshippers, for they are much frequented by beggars, and buyers and sellers, and barbers. The temples are so untidy, so full of rubbish. The gods are often in terrible disrepair. A god out-at-elbows, so to speak, or looking seedy, cannot inspire high thoughts, but he is all the people have to turn to and the fact that they turn to him, even in his painfully made-by-men condition, shows their hearts are longing for something beyond this world and greater than themselves.

The "Temple of the Eight Hundred Gods" seemed not so much a temple as a repository for gods. However, it was well-maintained, unlike others I had visited, and most of the gods had kindly, benevolent countenances, making it a much pleasanter place to visit. The god of fire had a bright red face and three eyes—the third being in his forehead and at right angles to the other two. Most of the peculiar things about the gods have a reason, so when I noticed one with a black hand, I inquired. Very often, these inquiries reveal interesting history, but this time, the answer was that he was being repaired and

when finished the hand would be a more natural colour for that divinity. The entrance to this temple was a perfect circle built out of stone, beautifully carved.

A temple with an attractive name was the Queen of Heaven Temple, but in fact it was singularly unattractive, being filthy. Barbers were plying their trade under the very nose of the goddess!

In China, the outside walls of temples are usually painted pink or yellow, so wherever those coloured walls are seen, a temple is indicated, although there may be temples with walls unpainted.

In all their Guild Houses they have a temple too, but these cannot be classed as public temples. The only Guild House I was in was the Shansi Bankers' Guild House in Shanghai, which is said to be the finest specimen of Chinese architecture in that city. It is certainly beautiful. The courtyards, made of stone, and with octagonal gates, make excellent photographs. When one sees these typical Chinese doorways for the first time, one exclaims, "How Oriental!" and they continue to strike one as genuinely picturesque. Entering the reception-hall with its tables, chairs, scrolls and opium couches, one finds everything clean. Now a clean place is so rare that it is worthy of comment. As this is a bankers' guild, the god of wealth occupies a prominent place along with his ministers, "Invite Riches" and "Gain Market." The shrine is red lacquered, touched here and there with gold, and all the accessories for temple worship are of the finest and kept in perfect condition.

There is another temple for the god of war, who may be called upon very soon to exert himself on behalf of his devotees, and between these is a theatre in an open court that is surrounded by galleries. Acting is done on a stage twelve feet high and the *leer-mong* gaze up from the courtyard where they stand, while the elite fill the galleries.

Last of all, the front entrance is reached. This is because, except at the anniversary of the birth and death of the god of war, the front doors are never opened and everyone must go around to the back. The stateliness of the entrance was somewhat marred by the stone floor being thickly strewn with pea-

42

nuts. My friend, an elderly lady, and I had two guides when we entered, but guides seemed to come from every turn and ere long we had a following of about twenty, not one of them able to speak English, but each expecting a *komshaw,* or tip, for his services. When we were a room or two from the exit our first guide said *komshaw,* so I laid on a table what money I thought was plenty for the service he had given and ignored the others; thereupon they attempted to block our way and every man demanded money. I straightened myself to my greatest height, five feet three inches, looked them square in the eyes, lifted my head, waved them aside, and when in utter amazement, they stepped back, I said to the trembling old lady, "Go on." When once we reached the street, she gasped, "How could you? I would have paid them all they wanted."

While in China, I always attended Chinese Church—Christian I mean, for although I could not understand, I could learn lessons by sight that could not be learnt elsewhere. The earnestness with which those Chinese who knew the gospel of Christ taught it to those of their countrymen who knew it not, was an inspiration to all missionary efforts. I wish those who think missions not worthwhile could have seen the faces of the teacher and the taught, the seeker and the doubter, and of the scornful who, in spite of his evident scorn, waited to hear more. One Sunday afternoon, I went with two Chinese ladies to a meeting for mill-workers held by a foreign missionary. The managers of the mill gave a room free of rent for this purpose because of the influence on the people. The room was filled long before the time for the meeting and although the personnel changed some, owing to obstreperous babies and irate people coming to the door and calling their relations away from the foreign devils, the room remained full to the end and many followed for some blocks as we were leaving. The mill-workers live in villages and these villages reminded me of the slums of New York, in the "Yiddish" quarter, for they were as densely populated and as crowded but not more so.

One little girl, not yet in her teens, enjoyed these meetings so much, judging from her face and from the heartiness of her singing, that I remarked on it to the missionary, who replied, "I am so glad she does for she has to work hard to support an opium-eating father." I thought then, if our children living in happy homes enjoy Sunday School as we know they do, how much more will these child-workers enjoy the only bright hour in their lives?

Chapter Four

In which Margaret talks of crows and graves as she rides a wheel-barrow through the countryside, continues her study of foreign missions and observes that young ladies the world over are swayed by fashion.

I had one more glimpse of the evangelical work of missions when I went with a missionary, who weighed over 200 pounds, to a village some miles distant from Shanghai. Why did I mention her weight? Because we had to ride on a wheel-barrow.

A Chinese wheelbarrow has a large wheel in the centre that invariably squeaks and on each side of the wheel is a shelf for passengers or freight. My more-than-200-pound friend sat on one side while I, of less than 100 pounds, sat on the other, and for the wheelman to balance us, it was necessary to tilt the barrow to an angle of 45 degrees with me on the down side continually slipping off. Each time we were bumped onto a single

long slab that answered for a bridge, I was fearful that it would
be the last time!

When we reached the nearest village, we were able to
engage another barrow and I rode with a Chinese woman of
about the same weight on the other side; then, wheelbarrow-
riding was nearly enjoyable. Whether to put the blame on the
wheelbarrow, the road or both, I knew not, but conditions
were such that my spectacles jiggled up and down on my nose,
keeping the landscape in perpetual motion; and my teeth
chattered as if I had been stricken with fear.

Although I could not speak Chinese and my companion
spoke no English, that was no hindrance to quite an animated
conversation. She would point to something, for example
some crows, and tell me the Chinese name, which I would
repeat and give her the English word; then, as at that moment

the crows flew away, I made a gesture indicating that action and said, "The crows are flying," thereupon she gave me the Chinese way of expressing that fact. Then, as I remarked before, my little knowledge of the Japanese language helped me to understand Chinese. Before coming to the East, whenever I heard the Chinese speaking, it seemed a confusion of sound out of which a single word could not be picked, but, owing to the training my ear has received in Japan, when in China, I could easily distinguish sounds although they rarely conveyed any meaning. Once, in a Chinese Church when a hymn was announced, I said to my friend, "is that not 276?" She was amazed, for I had been only two weeks in the country.

On this wheelbarrow trip, we did not leave Shanghai on these primitive conveyances, oh no! Only the *leer-mong,* use them there; we left in rickshas and drove out to the Arsenal where we were ferried across the Whang-poo. In this immense river, to protect the Arsenal, and for other purposes no doubt, were five Chinese warships of modern build and the few sailors we saw were fine looking men.

When once we crossed the Whang-poo, we were in real China, untouched by Shanghai fashions. This was my first trip into the country and everything was interesting, and the Chinese woman, in spite of neither understanding the other's language, gave me much information. We passed many kinds of graves; sometimes the coffin was exposed, wrapped in straw, and sometimes not; if the coffin were raised a few inches from the ground, then it meant that the inmate had died of smallpox and to tell me this, the Chinese woman, after drawing my attention to the fact that many coffins were raised, touched her face as if it were pitted. We passed temples that were exceedingly dirty and uninteresting; an outsider, such as I, would never suspect them of being temples were they not painted that peculiar reddish pink; then passed widows' monuments upon some of which the Chinese lavish their greatest skill. These are built, as the name indicates, to commemorate some noted woman. (I had always read of the down-trodden women of the East, but life among them revealed that they have great power in their world and are destined to still greater, for they have the necessary brain.)

We always had to abandon our wheelbarrow to walk through the villages because of the unevenness of the paved streets. Everywhere, Bible pictures, in the way of dress and custom, could be seen—indeed the man who so skillfully balanced our barrow looked as if he had stepped from the Old Testament.

Oh! the pity, that China should have gone so far so long ago and rested there! Especially when one remembers that gunpowder, printing and a host of other things originated in this land.

Another time, I went into the countryside with a missionary friend. News quickly spread of our arrival. I had been warned to expect a minute examination of my clothes—I got it. There was a clean little chapel in this village, with a bedroom off for the native preacher when he comes in his regular tour; into his room we were ushered. It had a wooden floor, a table, two chairs and a bed, so must be considered a nice room, that is, nice only by comparison, so I will not make any further comment on the room; besides, it was soon so full of people that hardly anything else could be seen in the subdued light that came through the oyster-shell window—subdued both by the oyster-shell and the grime of ages. While they were preparing our tiffin (luncheon), I taught a few English sentences to some and in return was taught a few in Chinese, and did all I could to make a favourable impression. I succeeded, for they expressed their sorrow that I could not address them. It was pleasing to notice that in many little ways, they tried to show honour to their missionary's friend. One way was that when the bowls of queer-looking food were brought in, there

47

was a fork and spoon for me. I debated which would be more polite, to use the fork and spoon, or use their "tools," the *qwa,* chopsticks. I decided on the chopsticks and they seemed pleased that I could manipulate them. We had brought tiffin with us but ate what they produced and left ours for them. The little chapel was crowded during the service; and although many came and went, still, a gratifying number remained during the whole service and seemed interested, and as if endeavouring to understand the meaning of this "Jesus' Religion," which is the name Christianity is known by. I saw little of the inside of mission work, for only those actually engaged in it know that side, but even the little I could see proved, in every way, that missions are worthwhile.

This was nowhere more apparent than in my visits to the mission schools. Here, the pupils have not only a full Western course but must also take the prescribed Chinese course and a systematic study of the Bible. Their knowledge of sacred history would put that of an ordinary Western Christian to shame. They may be strong heathen but still know the history of the Bible, and being forced to study high ideals must raise the standard of their lives.

The Chinese schoolgirl is very like her counterpart in Western countries; I mean in manner, not in dress, for a Chinese girl does not wear a skirt, but only long trousers of a gay colour and a short, tight coat of another gay colour (that is the fashion, at present, in Shanghai); her hair hangs in one long, thick, straight black braid down her back; where the hair first enters the braid it is wound round and round with coloured yarn and this same yarn puts in an appearance at the end of the braid. The hair over the forehead is fringed and fashion at present decrees that it must be cut to cover the forehead and hang down in front of the ears and must be curled—not what we would call curled, however, but merely a hump in it.

I was much amused when visiting a mission school where

ideals were so high that fashions were scorned, and speaking to one of the older pupils about the fashion of wearing a fringe, the missionary in charge said, "My girls know nothing of fashions." This was said in such a positive tone that I might have believed it had I not seen a conscious blush spread over the Chinese girl's face. I asked, "You do, don't you?" She replied, "Oh, yes, and I would like to follow the fashions." Women are women whether they be white or yellow, and girls are girls. The Chinese girls petitioned the Principal, on the United States Thanksgiving Day, for a holiday, saying how thankful they would be for it; they did not get it—showing that Principals are much the same the world over too. But instead, I addressed them, in English, of course, which the elder girls all understood when simply spoken, on the Opening of the Canadian Parliament, and the "Drawing-room." They were deeply interested, for as most of them belonged to official families, it might be within the range of possibility that some one of them might attend those functions; and I have no doubt that should any of them find themselves about to bow to the Governor-General and Her Excellency, they would go through that trying ordeal with the utmost composure.

The geography used in another school I visited states that the Chinese are "a half-civilized race," and when a Chinese teacher was imparting this to a class, she said, "Yes, that is true. Our women are not educated, and as they are about half of the population, so we are half-civilized." I thought that an intelligent observation and was further impressed by the school when I learned that six of the girls had just gone, in November, 1905, to the United States to enter upon university training, and one to study medicine in St. Louis.

Chapter Five

Wherein the importance of red as a bridal colour is impressed upon Margaret when she attends a fashionable wedding and a courteous act brings quiet praise.

Thanks to one of my mission friends, I had the privilege of being the only foreign guest at a Christian Chinese wedding with the old-time Chinese customs. A carriage was sent for us—us being a Chinese lady and myself. My companion, who was a cousin of the bride, had been educated in the United States and was taking an active part in her country's advancement. We were driven through the broad streets of Shanghai into narrow ones, and then into narrower still where we alighted at the entrance to the bridegroom's house. Here in the courtyard, we were received with a terrible clattering of so-called music—each guest on entering and on leaving was given this honour.

I do not remember, but no doubt, we sipped tea from covered cups before we were taken upstairs to see the presents. These, note, were displayed in the bridegroom's house. The bride's people are progressive, which accounts for the presents being nearly all foreign. They were wound around and around and criss-crossed with red yarn, reminding one of a spider-web party but that displayed a world of meaning to the Chinese. Everything possible connected with a wedding must be red. The presents evidently were greatly admired by the bridegroom who beamed as he showed them to us.

Again, I do not remember, but I am sure we must have sipped tea before we were allowed to leave, amid ear-splitting sounds of honour from the bride's house, which was only a few doors away. I said how convenient it was that the houses were so close together and was surprised to hear that the groom lived in the country, but the bride refused to go there to be married—no, indeed, his people were country bred and had no style, whereas she knew all the latest fashions and meant to make her wedding up-to-date (there is really so little difference between a Chinese girl and her sister in Western lands), so she compelled the bridegroom to rent this house near her home and furnish it especially for the occasion: yet, we read of the down-trodden women of the East.

When we arrived at the bride's home, her guests were feasting. She was sitting motionless at the head table dressed in a red gown, richly-embroidered, rented for the occasion, as was also the hat, a marvellous headgear somewhat resembling an umbrella made of red satin but heavily trimmed with imitation jade and pearls representing butterflies. Around the edge hung a fringe of pearls so thick that it could only be seen through when one string accidentally hung aslant. Beneath this remarkable hat, a red veil completely obscured the bride's face but allowed her to see through dimly, although she was supposed to be quite blind to what was going on (showing another resemblance to her Western sister).

When the feast was finished, the bride rose to retire to her room, where she changed her marvellous headgear for one of equal strangeness but suitable to wear to the church; thus, she prepared for her last trip as a maiden. A terrific clattering of gongs and shouting of men in the street heralded the coming of the bride's chair. The main reception-room of the house opened into a courtyard into which came the chair-bearers with the empty chair and crowds from the streets.

Public servants of the lower orders give as much trouble in China as elsewhere. Although these men brought the chair, they demanded high pay ere they would carry the bride to the church, and as that was obviously necessary, they got what they demanded. There was a great flutter of excitement when the chair arrived, but it had time to subside before the bride put in an appearance. She was coy. Some man in authority had to call, in beseeching terms, three times; then she felt that the demands of etiquette had been satisfied, so appeared in her changed headgear that resembled somewhat a bishop's hat, only very large.

In a Chinese house, her bright red dress and veil and her peculiar hat had seemed what one expected, but in the Anglican Church they were out of place. As in Western lands, the church was decorated with flowers. When the awful din announced the approach of the bride, the organ pealed forth (the organist being a Chinese girl) and the bride entered the church—not on the arm of her father—no, but guided by two women, professional managers for weddings, who were gowned in black to be as inconspicuous as possible, and one of whom walked backwards in front of the bride, holding her hands, and the other held her waist from behind. Slowly, the procession moved up the aisle. The bridegroom awaited his bride at the chancel steps.

Archdeacon Thompson performed the ceremony in English at the request of the bridal pair—all for style. It was a strange sight. A pretty orthodox Anglican Church, an audience mostly heathen, a venerable archdeacon in robes, a Christian bride in Oriental dress, the service in a tongue foreign to the contracting party, the solemn service preceded and followed by heathenish noises emblematic of what is desirable for marital bliss.

The ceremony over, the bride entered her chair and was carried through the streets. My Chinese friend and I entered our brougham and arrived before the bride at the groom's house. It seems that as long as the bride remains in her chair, she is considered to belong to her parents; but when once she steps out, then is the fatal step taken. She is then her husband's; so, naturally, she needed urging to come out of her chair, which was carried into the reception-hall of her husband's temporary home. Many people urged her in words no doubt coaxing, but she came not out until a young lady relative of her husband's brought her food and wine and requested her to come into the home prepared for her. The strangest part was that never once did the husband add his entreaties to those given; indeed, he appeared to be a disinterested party during most of the occasion.

However, when the bride emerged from her carriage (assisted ostentatiously by her managers), her husband joined

her and, side by side, they showed their veneration to the bridegroom's older relations. These honoured relatives, in turn, sat on two chairs over which were thrown red satin coverings. The method of showing respect was the same as used in ancestral worship—namely, prostrations on the part of the groom, but the bride's headgear prevented her from making any marked sign of respect.

The bride then went upstairs to change her hat for the one suitable for the feast that would soon take place. I was allowed upstairs and watched with keen interest the ceremony—and it was a ceremony—of hat changing, and I was glad that I could never be a Chinese bride. Her hair must be done in seven points; then, a thick ring of false hair is fastened on the top of her head and to this is pinned, in turn, the extraordinary hat, the whole being quite heavy, and no matter how much the managers hurt her when doing her hair, or fastening on hats, the bride must never show any sign of discomfort. Should she remonstrate because a pin was sticking into her head, or because one hair was pulling tighter than the others, her reputation would be marred; she would be classed by the neighbours as a shrew. The Chinese, naturally, wish to stand well among their neighbours and how things are conducted at a wedding settles the family's standing—though why they should care what the people thought who came swarming from the street, I cannot imagine, but they do. When I was told this, I hastily said that perhaps I had better leave, but was told that my presence indicated a certain distinction. It was amusing to see the style each family put on, neither willing to be outdone by the other, but I think the palm must be given to the bride's, for two of her guests (her gentlemen cousins) appeared in evening dress-suits of Western cut. I did not see these two gentlemen partaking of the feast of shark's fins and bird's nest soup with chopsticks; I wish I had. China is full of such contrasts.

The men and women do not eat in the same room. I was seated for the feast facing the courtyard, for the seat of honour must face to the heavens. The tables were about a yard square and of wood well polished by the constant wiping they receive. There were not any tablecloths, nor napkins, but after every meal hot wet towels are passed around upon which the hands and face are wiped. This was my first formal Chinese meal. I did not like some parts of it, but afterwards learned it had been cooked at a restaurant, which accounted for its greasiness. Chinese food properly cooked is good. I could live well on it, although I prefer my own. The Chinese use many kinds of meat and fowl. At this meal, I ate little and was afraid that I might give offence but my friend said that I would be considered polite. At subsequent dinner parties I never showed any such sign of good breeding, for I ate heartily and the taste of some of the good things is still with me.

The first thing served was hot wine in tiny cups holding merely a thimbleful. When the cups were refilled, I noticed the manner in which a guest held her cup. She slipped her fingers under it (there was no saucer), keeping her thumb tight to the palm of her hand, and as she lifted it, she slowly rose and received the replenishment standing, and then went through the performance backwards to regain her seat. I did the same. A smile passed over the whole company. My Chinese friend said, "You have pleased everybody." I am sure the flattery was sincere. It was a simple thing to do to give so much pleasure; but I find out here in the East that little courteous actions that are native, when done by a foreigner, give a peculiarly gratifying pleasure.

We left when the feast was finished and were escorted to the street door by the bridegroom. The celebration was not nearly over, there was yet to come the "teasing of the bride." It is just what the words mean and should the bride show any sign of impatience or annoyance, then the groom receives nothing but pity for having married so unrequiting a woman. We had wished to have seen the teasing process but we could not wait.

Chapter Six

In which Margaret sails on a sampan to ancient Soochow and the reader learns something of barges and household life on China's canals.

Interesting as things are in Shanghai, real China is not to be seen there. Knowing this, I was delighted to receive an invitation to visit Soochow. Soon, there will be a railroad running into Soochow: I was glad to get in ahead of the railway, for it brings so many foreign things in its wake. Now, in 1905, Soochow is reached by creeks and the Grand Canal. We were to depart from a creek in Shanghai that was full of navigating crafts and dirt of all kinds. In the low tide the junks were listing in the foul-smelling mud. I wished I could turn back without showing the white feather but that was not possible. A narrow springing plank led from the bank to one of a row of barges for the transportation of passengers into the interior. Passengers crossed the reeking mud on this and were preceded and followed by strange-looking bundles—baggage is very much bundled here. We had each a *pookay* (bedding wrapt in matting, a huge unwieldy bundle); then there was the tiffin basket, which must necessarily be an ample one, for no-one is sure when starting out on a journey that the end will be reached at the expected time; a lamp, which when hung from the ceiling, cast a weird light on everything; a chair, which is a luxury, for the bed-shelf can always be used for a chair if one does not require to lean back, nor mind one's feet dangling in the air as in childhood days. Then, add this to toilet articles, and personal baggage, and parcels and boxes taken to oblige friends, and then one realizes what a burden are those infinite necessities induced by the civilization that we are forcing upon these Eastern peoples.

After safely crossing on this narrow plank, we walked along a foot-wide shelf that ran around the barge until we came to the hole we were to crawl through to enter our stateroom—I use that word not knowing the Chinese one that must surely be more appropriate, for there was no state and little room. The light in this room is dim compared to the brilliant sunshine outside. The doorway and small windows are darkened by the *pookays* and other bundles waiting to be passed inside. In they come, you step back, and back further, putting yourself into the smallest possible space. When everything is inside, the servants (it is impossible to travel in China with any degree of comfort without at least one servant; in fact, a servant is a necessity) begin the stowing-away process and gradually, you allow yourself to expand and when everything is settled, you are amazed to find ample room and every prospect of comfort. The room is clean, for there is nothing in it but what you brought, save the four walls painted white and on each side a shelf of woven hemp for a bed.

I had heard that coolies, particularly those along the waterways, who were of low class, expressed themselves in quite unacceptable language. Although I am not cognizant of swearing, it would be easily discernible and I expected my ears to be polluted with oaths and quarrels and to see some fighting. But not at all. Out of that jam of boats, we moved slowly and peacefully amid happy sounds—it may be that the Chinese are, as the Japanese, without "cuss words."

My servant could not speak English, nor I Chinese, but as

she was my friend's trusted *amah,* she felt the responsibility of having me in her charge. According to Chinese custom, I was "put on her body." She would politely ask me some question, in Chinese, that required sentences to express. I would listen, of course not understanding a word, and when she finished, I would gravely answer in English. This over, she would proceed to do what she had questioned me about, while keeping an eye on me to see that the action met with approval. Language is often-times unnecessary. It is surprising how one can manage without the language of words if there be language of sign, or motion, and a mutual sympathy.

One night is the length of time it usually takes to go from Shanghai to Soochow. And in the morning as the servant is tending your many necessities, you crawl up through the hole to see the country and get some fresh morning air, and are amazed to find that all night long the roof over your head has been packed closely with Chinese passengers. These passengers lie on the roof, in astonishing numbers, each wrapped in a blanket. Queer-shaped, bright blue rolls would suddenly seem to contain life; there would be a wiggling motion and then a gradual unfolding until a sleepy face would appear and then an arm would reach out for the ever-present teapot.

Soon after turning into the Grand Canal, we could see Soochow in the distance; it looked like many notes of exclamation, the long stroke being the pagodas, and the periods the small native houses. One by one as the pagodas came into view, they were named to me, the Big Pagoda, the Old Pagoda, the Twin Pagodas, the Pen and Ink Pagodas, and so on. The word "pagoda" means, "House of Idols," "The Holy House." The Pen and Ink Pagodas have an interesting history. The Pen Pagoda was built first for some god because of the gratitude of the people to this god, but it would have been better had they not so expressed themselves, for the god, like many deities of the human sort, getting a little, wanted more; in other words, waxed indignant that he had only been given a pen; of what use was a pen without ink? So he sent an epidemic. At first, people knew not why sickness and death were laying such a heavy hand on them, but after consultation with geomancers who mediate between the gods and man, it was revealed the why and wherefore of the god's anger. A subscription was taken for the building of an Ink Pagoda and contributions came from some of the wealthiest and most influential men in Soochow.

Soochow is a great city and like others of its kind, its commerce is met with long ere the city is reached. Curious unwieldy junks with high square walled-up sterns and nothing to speak of for a bow except an eye, some of which are realistically painted; others are known to be eyes because that is the place for the eye. These boats with the eye are from Ning-po, for the man of that province says "no have eye, no can see, no can see, no can walk, no can walk, no can go." That settles the matter. Occasionally, there would be a mandarin's boat elaborately carved and fitted with marble and rosewood. No foreign-built boats were to be seen. The canals throughout the country are guarded by gun-boats. What funny things they are! Small boats, each with a small gun on the stern so that they could only shoot when retreating—the guns had the appearance of not being able to do much damage—if indeed they could be put through the formality of firing.

We had to pass Customs, which consisted in signing our names in a book. Customs in China are a great nuisance. Naturally, one expects Customs on landing in a country but does not expect to meet them on every little trip, in season and out of season. My friend sent two pounds of candy from Shanghai to Hankow and had to pay 20¢ duty; fortunately, the sender can pay the duty. At the Customs, boats called sampans crowded around our tow of barges, the owners thereof shouting for passengers; judging from the sounds, there must be a stereotype phrase but all that I could understand was "lay," "come." We came, so thankful to leave the crowded barge and get on a boat. This was of such peculiar build that it was necessary to back into it, so small was the opening, and it was equally necessary to bang one's head and lose one's temper, but we were the only passengers, which was its great attraction. The crew was a man, his wife, a baby and a small boy tethered to avoid the trouble of having to pull him out of the water had he been free to wander. Oftentimes Chinese will not rescue a drowning person because if they do that person is "on the body of his rescuer," and that is a serious matter, for it means that the rescuer is responsible for the rescued as long as he lives. A stupid idea, sure enough.

Having heard that the women of China were down-trodden and finding it not true in regard to all of the better class, I thought surely it applied to the lower classes; but here, on this little boat, the woman was the chief mariner and her word was law. These women mariners are remarkable beings. A compound of man at the wheel and woman at the hearth. When not rowing or directing affairs outside they are within, cooking, washing or dressing the baby. Their clothing is scant, their feet bare and their sleek black hair is always ornamented as best they can afford; sometimes it may be only by a piece of red yarn, or a metal head-scratcher. (It amused me to see even ladies wearing these head-scratchers stuck in their hair so as to be handy.)

The whole family live in the boat. The hooded tunnel in the centre is, by day, a place for passengers, and by night, a house for the nautical family. We chose our sampan because the family was few and our belongings were many, but the sampans where the family was larger presented strange sights. Here would be a woman standing at the tiller with a baby strapped to her back; there, a woman rowing with graceful movement as she rocked to and fro, making her sampan dart in and out with wonderful accuracy through the miscellany of craft, and everywhere children leaning out of the windows and over the edge in perilous positions. The family cat prowling from bow to stern; hens trying to pick up a living; clothes hanging out to dry as if the deck were a backyard; things dangling from the stern of the boat because there is no room on board.

In the daytime, life abounded on the canals; there was motion everywhere. At night, all was still; human beings of the boating population were huddled under the hoods of their boats and were resting after the day's work and the dying glimmer of a fire in a brazier on the poop showed where the simple evening meal had been cooked.

It was early morning when we lowered ourselves into the small hooded part of the sampan and had our baggage piled high fore and aft until it was impossible to see out except through the queer little opening in the side of the hood called, by courtesy, a window. The motion of these sampans is a wondrous encouragement to seasickness. We passed through the water gate of the old wall, built 2200 years ago and into the ancient, aristocratic and beautiful city of Soochow.

The canals are in a splendid state of preservation, but much too narrow and crooked for the speed that modern times demand. In the interior of China, it is advisable not to expect evidences of progress but to drift with the tide of human affairs, for by so doing, one may not reach one's destination quite as quickly, but certainly in a pleasanter frame of mind. Disruptions will happen, frequently causing the remainder of the journey to be continued by land. The city is intersected by these canals and instead of stepping into a carriage, one steps into a boat; or if the way be not near a canal, one is borne on a sedan chair. In the city, the streets are too narrow for even a *jinrikisha*.

One objection foreigners living in Soochow have to travelling on the canals is the disgusting smell, but to me, whether to go by land or water is merely Hobson's Choice. It is impossible to escape the vile odours, for street and canal alike are used for sewers. Add to this the smells coming from the waste carried in open buckets slung on long bamboo poles over the shoulders of coolies. Frequently the odourous contents spill plentifully as the waste is carried to a scow resting in the canal. When the scow is filled with this waste, and that dredged from the bottom of the canal, it then travels into the country, uncomposted, to be used as fertilizer for vegetable and grain fields. These fertilizers in their raw condition are a grave menace to health and Oriental civilization must be subject to to a heavy discount until this use of uncomposted manure is prohibited. Foreigners living in China and Japan know this, yet they will eat uncooked vegetables and then blame the climate when they become sick.

If one becomes sick in this country, it could be risky as medical practice on the Chinese plan is peculiar. Generally speaking, what cures one is expected to cure all, but what kills one is not expected to kill another, for it is tried again and again. I heard of one Chinese doctor who had reached such fame that he saw patients only from 9 to 12 o'clock in the night and then saw only ten each night; the eleventh (whether the case was acute or chronic did not seem to matter) was given a ticket so that he would be the first seen the next night.

Chapter Seven

On the streets of Soochow, Margaret endures slippery walking and debates the merits of different paving-stones. She makes a wise purchase and climbs a pagoda. Outside Soochow, she sees the fate of unwanted babies.

But I must not dwell too long on ill-health and smells for Soochow is a beautiful city and there is a Chinese proverb that says "heaven above and Hanchow and Soochow below." One of the pleasant sights here are the little donkeys, half the height of any donkey I have ever seen, running along the streets wearing strings of bells around their necks making a merry sound, suggesting sleigh bells, although there is not much else to support the thought. One often sees a big Chinaman sitting on one of those miniature donkeys, quite unconscious that the fitness of things would be better sustained if he carried the donkey. One tall foreigner whom I knew said whenever he rode a donkey and wished to rest the donkey from the burden of his weight, he just let down his legs and walked without ever stopping the beast.

In Soochow, some of the streets are unpaved and they are quagmires owing to the perpetual carelessness of the water-carriers as they go to and fro from the public wells to their customers' homes. Fortunately, most of the streets are paved with either cobblestones or long slabs of granite. When walking on these slabs, worn slippery by countless millions of feet that have passed over them in 2200 years of the city, one longs to return to the cobblestones; but when these are reached and found to be slippery too from the constant spilling of liquids that are carried in a bobbing fashion from bamboo poles and the splashing of water from thousands of buckets, one thinks again of preference for the slab-paved streets.

I am not the only one who has difficulty with footing on wet streets. Chinese men on rainy days wear leather shoes with great metal wedges fastened on the soles. One day, hearing a company of soldiers tramping behind me, I thought it wise to step into a doorway to let the group pass—the company of soldiers turned out to be one man in rain shoes on the stone pavement.

The principal shopping street is paved with cobblestones. There was an agitation to have cobblestones replaced by slabs but when the spirits were consulted through the medium of wily geomancers—bear in mind the spirits must be consulted on every occasion—it was found that the change would be disastrous, for, were the slabs laid, the dragon that lives stretched under the street with his head in, or under, the Confucian Temple at one end, and his tail in, or under, a pagoda at the other end, would be unable to turn over and, in his anger at this situation, he would send calamity of some sort on the people; hence the street remained cobble. This street was originally six feet wide, but each shopkeeper takes as much off for the display of his wares as the law allows, or rather does not disallow. The government is lenient to these trespassers so long as a mandarin's chair and suite can pass unhindered. Mandarins think they make an imposing array as they pass through the streets, and maybe they do in the eyes of their compatriots, but aliens laugh. The attendants' horses, always white and always dirty and ungroomed, and mounted by men who ride as if they were afraid, are ludicrous and made more so if by chance, the self-satisfied face of the official inside the chair is seen.

The day I was on this street was bargain-day and as usual, it was the opposite to a Western bargain-day, for the shopkeepers were turning over their goods in the front part of their windowless and doorless stores, and in high falsetto, that is thought to be very winning, were proclaiming the great value for little money that their bargains represented; no crowd surrounded them; no crowd blocked the way, possibly because a queer looking little foreigner on the street was a greater sight. Certainly I had a following that completely blocked the way every time I stopped to look at the wares displayed. They

would crowd in on me and I would turn first to one side, then to the other, and wave them back, saying quietly in English, which of course, none understood, "stand back, stand back there," and they would stand back. On my return to where I was visiting, I told this to my friends and they said they never would have dared to do such a thing. Why? I know not.

One day when I was accompanied by two servants, neither of whom could speak English, I saw in a shop what, for months I had been looking for in the East, an incense burner in bronze—which in its manufacture, when it is red hot, has gold "thrown in" upon its surface. That I could not speak the language of the people around me and that they could not speak mine did not prevent me from bargaining for this incense burner.

Negotiations opened by my pointing to the burner and then to the counter near me, but many gestures were required ere the right burner was transferred from shelf to counter. It was in use, so was partly filled with ashes and in it was a small remnant of incense. Wishing to know the price, I laid a Mexican dollar, which money is used in some parts of China, beside it. When the man uttered some queer sounds I knew, from knowledge of the Japanese language, that he meant six dollars, but to make sure, raised six fingers and then after receiving an affirmative nod, I jingled my dollar, indicating that was my offer. Thereupon, he, in disgust at my meanness or little appreciation of the burner's true value, replaced it on its high shelf as if to end the business. But I was there to buy that very thing, and by gestures had it brought back.

A conversation, consisting of language that only one understood and gestures that both understood, flowed freely. In course of time he came down a dollar and I went up one, but still the coveted bronze was not mine. Near despair at the thought of having to meet his price but deriving great pleasure from the strangeness of the situation, I spied a slight flaw and by gravely shaking my head and by a plentiful sprinkling of "Tut-tut-tuts" in the proper tone, I noticed the first sign of relenting on his part, for he tried to rub off the flaw. And then another sign that I was near the price was that he consulted his companion. I was quick to grasp this and found more and more blemishes. I could not tell him, if I would, that these flaws made it more valuable to me, as then I felt it was more likely to be genuine, for China is not much behind in the matter of fraudulent imitation. His reluctance, I am afraid, intoxicated me and I lost my head and offered 50¢ more; thereupon he clapped his hands, showing that the deal was closed. My friends, who could read Chinese, read the trademark and on it were the words for Ming Dynasty,* so I, who never pride myself on buying wonderful things for a song, or owning things of antiquity, now possessed a much coveted piece from the Ming Dynasty, having acquired it for the mythical song.

There is a pagoda at the end of this business street, as I

mentioned earlier. I climbed as far as the fifth storey, going out on the balcony at each storey to view the city and the country. The course of the Grand Canal could be traced for miles and everywhere that day sunshine was over the city and not in it. Streets could not be seen from above, so slit-like were they, and below, a crust of roofs extended on every hand almost to the wall.

On that old grey, grim wall that circles the city so majestically, the air is fresh and sweet as it blows from the mountains that lie a short distance away. There is no sound of the countless ear-splitting noises of the city. There is a monastic silence broken only by the cawing of innumerable birds. Built two centuries before Christ, the wall is twelve miles in circumference. On the outside there is a sheer drop of 60 feet and on the inside, it is banked with earth to within six feet of the top.

Looking down from the pagoda, I wondered what would be seen if the crust of roofs was suddenly to be raised. It would be somewhat as if a large stone that covered an anthill was turned over, with crowds scurrying hither and thither. As I write this "anthill idea" it occurs to me that it is a fit description of New York's busy streets also, but what a difference!

Sunshine does not penetrate into the streets below because they are so narrow, and flanked on either side by high buildings from which hang, close together, enormous wooden signs; and to show that the Chinese have no idea of the value of sunshine, the streets are often roofed over with matting, picturesque but unsanitary. Many industries are carried on in those streets, and gambling everywhere. A small boy cannot buy a cash of candy without throwing dice for it, or turning a wheel of fortune: one cash hazarded and lost, another must go, and so on; the old story.

But from high on the pagoda, you do not see these details, you see below a city with thousands of roofs. It was a strange sight, that old, old land recalling again and again Biblical scenes.

Pagodas I understand are usually of odd-numbered storeys; this one had nine and they all bring good luck. Suddenly I decided it might not mean good luck for me if I remained there longer, for more than a dozen Chinese had followed me on to the balcony and if one of them thought he would be doing his country honour by putting one little foreigner out of existence, he easily could have done so by throwing me over into space; so when a disturbing noise inside of the pagoda told me that more Chinamen were coming up I hastily departed. I never like showing the white feather but it was only that morning that I had heard for the first time of the strong anti-foreign feeling that was in Soochow, and indeed, that Soochow was a hot-bed of anti-foreign feeling and excited meetings were held every day.

My fears were well-founded, for it was afterwards considered too dangerous for ladies to go walking upon the streets. We walked, as quickly as possible, which at best was but slowly, so crowded were the crooked, uneven streets choked overhead with countless fantastic wooden signboards, which, in the early twilight looked weird, making good subjects for imagination to work upon; walked over bridges that were six or eight steps higher than the street and on which were temporarily stationed travelling kitchens, refreshment stalls and pedlars displaying their miscellaneous collections, fairly under the passerby's feet. We passed policemen occasionally whose manner said, in capital letters, "Don't depend on me;" passed public menders of clothes plying their needles whilst sitting on bamboo stools in the street; then stepped into a shop to let a sedan chair pass, following which ancient chair was a bicycle ridden by a long-gowned Chinaman with his pigtail floating out behind. We had to go through spiked thief-gates, which a few hours later would be closed, thus dividing the whole city into sections so that thieves had little chance of escaping. Even people of honest intention had difficulty going from one part of the town to another, for at each thief-gate, the watchmen who slept in a wretched dog-kennel had to be aroused from a deep sleep and could be awakened only if perseverance were practised. Temptation was strong to dally here and there to see strange sights but discretion said to hurry on, and really I was thankful to step inside the mission compound.

I fully expected to return many times to that business street with its pagoda, but I never did. It would be as much as my life was worth to do so. Ah! you think that an exaggeration? It is not. One week from the day I was surrounded by the *leermong*, whom I had to wave back every few minutes as I bargained for the bronze, the missionaries with whom I was visiting were telegraphed by their consul—the United States Consul in Shanghai—to flee for their lives. I left Soochow three days before this telegram was sent, thus missing the experience of having to flee for my life from an old walled Chinese city. But if I had had the experience, I should have missed being caught downtown in the Shanghai Riots. Which? oh which would I have preferred to have missed? I cannot decide.

That night as I was dropping off to sleep there was a fiendish noise, which made my hair rise up on end and my flesh creep. It seemed to be on our compound and we were three women alone and no men. A door slammed and shook the house. Visions of what I had seen during the day came in rapid succession to my mind. Eventually, reason asserted itself and told me that this noise was merry-making in connection with a wedding, December being the month for weddings, but reason does not make one's hair lie down, nor stop one's teeth from chattering, nor make one's flesh resume its proper calm.

Across the Grand Canal, and outside the ancient wall of the old city, is the comparatively new part of Soochow. Here, following the canal for five miles, is a driveway for carriages. This is where I saw a purely Chinese institution, a building which accepts unwanted babies.* As a rule, babies here are thrown away only because of the superstition that in some way, she will bring bad luck. I say "she" for of course it is never necessary to throw away a boy. In the front of the building there is a big drawer in which the baby is deposited. After the baby has been put in and the drawer shut, a bell is rung to inform those inside of its presence. The baby is retrieved, raised from infancy and then sold as a slave. All well-to-do Chinese families have slaves. I would have liked to have opened this drawer to see what it was like inside, but I was in the company of others on the Grand Canal.

*MacLean's friends may have been mistaken as the bronze burner should have had a reign mark as well as a dynasty mark.

*Possibly a *Shang-Tang* (Hall of Good Things), a benevolent institution dating back to Han times.

Chapter Eight

In which Margaret explores the mysteries of gardens and funerals; is received in a 300-room mansion complete with head wives, little wives and slaves, and there is given silk slippers. These last bring reflections on foot-binding.

It was an ideal afternoon, the sky clear, the sun bright, the air cool and comparatively fresh, the sights along the way picturesque and strange. Great *pailous* (ceremonial gateways) or monuments built to commemorate noted widows, I'm told, loomed up, their magnificent proportions and carvings clear-cut against the sky, oftentimes making a frame for a beautiful natural picture. Stone bridges built in a semi-circle, the circle being completed in the reflection, added their quota to the pleasure of the trip.

At length we arrived at the garden we were to visit. A Chinese garden is far removed from any Occidental idea of a garden. A foreigner may walk through one and see it outwardly, but to understand requires as close a study as is necessary to learn the language, closer even, for these gardens embody the ideals of the Chinese. They are essentially a place for reflection and communion. I felt as if in the presence of a great mystery. Everywhere right at hand there was something, if only one's eyes were opened to see. To one having no knowledge of Oriental life, the garden was only odd combinations of lava and rock, little ponds spanned by zigzag bridges, paths neatly tiled, with days and days of labour, possible only in a country where labour is cheap; the pieces of tile and broken dishes bought for the purpose were turned on edge and laid in patterns.

But one has only to live a short time in the East to know that everything of this sort has meaning and that nothing is done on the hit-or-miss plan. Every detail is governed by a rule; there are rules for perspective and proportion, and these are strictly adhered to, although at first one is inclined to think there are no such lines. The patterns in the tiled paths mean happiness, long life (the wish is always that you may live a thousand years), wealth, and so on; and the zigzag paths are designed to counter the evil spirits.

As summer-houses form a feature of Occidental gardens, so rooms do in Oriental gardens. These rooms are built of white plaster and the wood used in them is of a rich brown colour. The entrances are pear-shaped, or round, or square, or octagonal, and in every case built of stone. Window spaces are usually filled in with open designs of porcelain, sometimes representing bamboo, sometimes in geometrical designs; occasionally though, there will be one of quaint shape, without any filling, from which you may be sure a view of a great beauty is to be seen. Outside of this window, there are mountains, frightful in their ruggedness, which may be scaled by narrow trails; there are gorges and ravines crossed by dangerous-looking bridges; there cataracts fall into rivers that flow for such a distance that the current is lost and lakes are formed, where grotesque goldfish disport; and all this in a space a yard or two square.

There is a large library, many sitting rooms and dining-rooms and two theatres in this garden; and these at New Year's time are in great demand. We took tea in an octagonal room overlooking a pond in which the lotus, a Buddhist emblem, grew. As the lotus lifts its buds out of the slimy ground, to a greater or lesser height above the water, unfolding its leaves and flowers upon whose spotless petals no traces can be seen of the mire from which it springs, so the soul of man must rise from the slime of sin, by its own power and efforts, to greater heights and reach the blessedness of Nirvana.

The literary tastes of the guests are met by quotations from the classics hanging upon the walls of the different rooms, while straight-backed, antique-looking, blackwood chairs, tables and opium sofas to match were chained to the floors so that the taste of the casual kleptomaniac could not be gratified. I was sorry to leave, feeling that I understood so little of what I saw, and knowing that although I could see I was blind to much of the beauty and blind entirely to the meaning.

Usually I have no desire to see places by moonlight, as I much prefer my bed; but I had a great longing to see that garden by the light of a full moon. There was a moon that night which, as we were slowly rowed homeward, cast its rays in a broad path along the Grand Canal and touched the *pailous* which now loomed up in giant proportions against the sky, bridges that now appeared to be circular and junks and sampans, with its transforming light. The western sky was still aglow with the setting sun and against it, the old wall with its crenellated parapet, its gate-towers and its dignity of age, was majestic. It was evening and the canal was quiet; in the boats under their hood of matting the family had gathered, and here and there a flickering light of prepared string in oil showed that the inmates had not yet gone to sleep.

I have endeavoured to describe the outside of a Chinese city, and now shall try to tell something of the inside, or of the home life and the homes. Knowing that Soochow was an aristocratic city, I wondered where could the aristocrats live? With this question in my mind, I stepped into a sedan chair that was lined with pale blue silk piped with dark blue and had yellow silk curtains at the windows; outside all around hung a deep, dark-coloured fringe that swayed in unison with the chair as I was carried through the streets on the shoulders of two men with a third running ahead shouting, "Clear the way," or rather, the Chinese equivalent. About every block, the out-runner would relieve one of his companions from the burden of the chair and this was done by a great swing in the air as the chair was heaved from one man to the other. For my own peace of mind I thought it best not to inquire as to the ratio of accidents at this critical time. My friend in her chair followed. In her chair, beneath her feet, was a brass foot-stove.

We turned into a street at an unfortunate time, for we broke into the middle of an immense funeral and people gathered to watch the procession seemed to think we belonged to it. There were all sorts of queer-looking things and queerly dressed people who were no doubt proper for a funeral. It would have been intensely interesting to have stood by and watched it passing; but as it was, we could only see a part of it. It was all so strange that I cannot remember anything distinctly; there was a medley of catafalque, big umbrellas and gay colours. I had seen one or two simple funerals in Shanghai where the humble mourners rode on wheelbarrows or walked, where the coffin was of logs cemented together, borne to its resting place suspended by ropes and poles from coolies' shoulders. The only guard against the Evil Spirit was one gong, but that gong was always put to good use and made enough noise to deafen onlookers if not the Evil Spirit.

What I am about to say concerning death and its accompaniments in China is only from reading or hearsay. I learned that a coffin is a much valued present. Happy indeed is the Chinaman who has his coffin ready and in his house awaiting the day that must come. I heard of one old man who was being badly treated but he bore it all knowing that his coffin was ready for him; the grossest ill-treatment of him was the stealing of his coffin. He was heartbroken. A foreigner happened to hear of this and bought the poor old man a new coffin and had it chained to the floor. In due time, this poor old man died and it was found he owned valuable lands, all of which he left to the foreigner who had bought him his coffin. I did not see any poor coffinless men to be kind to, alas!

When a Sovereign dies, the whole nation goes into mourning: no-one is allowed to shave for one hundred days—poor barbers, how hard on them! Signs of mourning are everywhere then; even the wheelbarrows have blue cushions instead of red ones. White and sack-cloth is for the deepest mourning; blue for half mourning. A Chinaman wears mourning for his superiors or equals, but not necessarily for his wife. When women mourn, they must sit on the ground or, worse still, the cold stone floors of their houses for seven days and sleep on mats near the coffin. During these days food is not cooked, chopsticks are not used, as deepest sorrow is symbolized by using the hands for conveying food to the mouth.

It is a most expensive matter for a rich Chinaman to die. A poor man can die, and a happy resting-place can quickly be found that will bring harm neither to himself nor his relations. Not so with the rich man. The gods must be consulted, the spirits in general, the particular spirits of that man's ancestors, as well as the living descendants. All must be consulted and all must agree on the final resting-place. This takes time, sometimes years. Meanwhile, the confined body stays in the house. And it takes money—for the spirits can only be reached through professional mediums who are specialists and demand specialists' prices gauged by the wealth of the family. There is honour in a long delay of burial if caused by profound reflection, infinite inquiry and much communication with the mysterious Fung-shui, which teaches that the whole earth is alive with influences that affect, for good or evil, the living as well as the dead. During the time for mourning no silk clothes are worn; after the deepest mourning, sackcloth is discarded, but white is worn, then blue. If you see a man with a white button on his hat and a white cord woven into his queue he is in deep mourning; if the button be blue then it is second mourning.

Progressive Chinese are trying to cut down the expenses connected with weddings and funerals but it will be a long time before funeral costs are cut to any extent, for superstition has laid its clutches deep into the soul of the Chinese.

The day that we got into the funeral procession mentioned earlier, we were on our way to call at a magnificent Mohammedan home and passed through many streets. In one, we saw a steamer trunk dangling from one end of a pole slung across a coolie's shoulder, while on the other end of the pole hung a *pookay.* To my surprise, I recognized these as my property being conveyed to my new place of residence.

In a street as narrow as the others, we stopped at an unpretentious gate in a high, plastered, black-painted wall. The gate was opened immediately, for we were expected. My friend that morning had sent her husband's card asking permission to call in the afternoon. The card was a thin piece of paper, bright red on the front with the name printed in black Chinese characters and white on the reverse. One calls in the afternoons as Chinese ladies do not rise until noon, and then take a long time to dress.

This friend, who so kindly took me into the homes of the people of China, is the wife of a medical missionary and devotes her time to the social life of the Chinese people, calling on them, accepting their invitations, and inviting and receiving them in her home—an important and profitable vocation from a missionary standpoint, for it brings them into the outer circle of Christian influence and seeing that the Christians' homes are not the dreadful place they have been told about, they gradually come within to the inner circles. This lady being born in China and having learnt the language in childhood, has no difficulty conversing with the people, and having a charming, tactful manner, and social tendencies, makes an ideal person for that difficult position.

No word suits the motion of the Chinese sedan chair better than the word "jellied," so, we jellied through this common-looking gate into an outer room—a "stable" for sedan chairs—then on through a courtyard and an entrance hall, then another courtyard, and looking ahead, as doors flew open, there was a beautiful vista of reception-halls and court-yards alternately, ending in a brilliantly lit place of honour. Had this been a Confucian or Buddhist Chinese home, in the place of honour would have been ancestral tablets; but being Mohammedan, there was a selection from the Koran written in blue on a white tile and a valuable painting—called, by the Japanese, *kakemono*—and a costly ornament. After jellying through five or six reception-halls and courtyards our chairs were lowered and we stepped out upon a stone floor.

This, like all reception-halls, had a domed roof of very dark, reddish brown wood inset with oyster shells, scraped thin to let in light. The two outer walls were a series of double-

leafed French doors, closely latticed with the dark wood to hold the shell lights: the light, toned down by the oyster shells through which it passes, softens the gay colouring of the men's and women's clothing, and adds much to the splendour of the environment. This house is an exceptional one, and perhaps is the largest in Soochow; it might well be, for it has 300 rooms. Oriental splendour in truth.

The house was spotlessly clean, for the owners were Mohammedans. It had sunny courtyards with fountains and gardens, lofty chambers with exquisitely carved woodwork, marble floors, tables and chairs rich in colouring and inset with marble, the design of forest and mountain formed by the natural stratum of the stone, and wall-paintings done in watercolours with the freshness of nature preserved. When I saw this beautiful home and recalled the streets through which we had come, I no longer felt sorry that the Chinese ladies were kept in their homes and could not go on the streets. Home was by far the best place if there be courtyards, and sunshine, and fountains; but how many homes are there like that! Few, ah, few indeed! This was one of the first Chinese homes I was in, and after going into others, I could not but think, if the ladies of China had been in the habit of walking on the streets the streets would not be as they are. Would not the streets of Occidental cities degenerate if ladies never went upon them? One never sees a lady on the streets in China; not even riding in a sedan chair, for then the blinds are drawn and she sees not, neither is she seen. A Chinese lady does not have a round of afternoon calls to make, or evening entertainments to attend, for as far as I could find out, there is no mingling of families in a social way. On such occasions as weddings and birthday feasts the relations are invited but not outsiders, privileged foreigners excepted.

This family of Mohammedans had lived so long in China that, to my untrained eye, they were the same as the Chinese, save that the men assisted their wives in receiving us, which the Chinese do not. We were taken from one grand reception-room to another, stopping to sip tea out of the covered cups in which it is made. To do this it is necessary to lift the lid and with it gently push back the tea leaves, then replace the lid on a slant and gracefully, if you can, sip the tea that comes through between the lid and the cup. A novice usually succeeds in having two or three streams flowing elsewhere than where they should. My friend's nose was too advanced to use the cup in the orthodox fashion, so she had to remove the lid and drink from the bowl—I say bowl for it is not our idea of a cup, having no handle.

Only about twenty people of the family followed us on our tour of inspection. There were the gentlemen of the house in gay clothing—Chinese men adopt en masse all the tints of a Canadian sunset—one wore peach-coloured trousers and sky-blue tunic with pipings and trimmings of other colours. Besides the men there were head wives in handsome brocaded coats and heavily embroidered, red silk skirts, and with pearls and jade ornamenting the flaps that form something of an apology for a cap, and with gold ornaments in their hair, and bracelets on the wrists; little wives plainly dressed and without ornaments; little girls with cheeks painted pink to represent the flush of youth, but the windows of the soul showed what suffering they were enduring with their bound feet; boys bright-eyed and alert, so evidently the darlings of the family and so like boys in our home land, for when sent off to their room to their tutor, they returned saying the teacher could not be found—and after all, foreigners were visiting at the home. Most delightful of all were the babies, for a Chinese baby is altogether a funny looking object in his winter clothes, which are padded; and, as he is naturally fat, it is sometimes difficult to tell which way he is longest. His scanty hair, gathered into an embryo pigtail, encouraged to hope for greater things by a liberal use of red yarn, is enough to make anyone smile. Then, of course, servants and slaves came and went.

There were thirteen departments in this household; that is, all the thirteen men of the family lived there, each with his head wife, his little wives, children, servants and slaves. My friends asked how many children were in the household, but no-one knew off-hand, and not having an abacus handy to reckon on, no attempt was made to count the number. I taught a few phrases of English to one of the little boys, one of which he remembered to repeat as I was leaving: it was, "Goodbye, come back again."

These people were exceedingly kind in showing us their house; we were even taken into bedrooms, almost as cheerless as the reception-rooms, though not quite, for the floors were of wood, painted a warm, reddish brown. A Chinese bed is an important piece of furniture, as so much ceremony is connected with it. A bride makes hideous-looking ornaments for her bed that are full of meaning and if not properly made or properly hung would bring bad luck in the thousand forms in which it can come to a Chinese. As a piece of furniture, a Chinese bed may be very handsome. It has a canopy of wood artistically carved and inset with marble; at each end, small drawers are inset into the base. There are no springs, but instead bands of hemp are woven across the frame of the bed to support the mattress. The Chinese use low pillows—much the same as ours. I wish I could remember if they use sheets but I cannot.

Inside of the carved woodwork that supports the canopy hang curtains, which are drawn at night so that the sleeper is completely shut in—a very good idea in a land where mosquitoes are plentiful, but at variance with our idea of ventilation while sleeping.

We were shown into a room where there was a sick woman. The room was darkened by red curtains and the bed hung with red. Seeing this, I remembered reading that in Ireland, for certain ailments the room and bed are darkened with red, and thought it strange that the same peculiar custom should exist in two countries so far apart and so dissimilar. At the back of the bed stood a low table with a lighted candle on it—is that the custom too in Ireland? The canopy made the bed like a small room, at night the curtains surrounded the bed, in the day they were looped back at the front.

They had kept the room that they were most proud of until the last; it was a foreign room. "Ah! A foreign room," we exclaimed. They beamed.

It was supposed to be a dining-room, for in the centre was a long dining-table but on top of the dining-table was a white bedspread and on top of the bedspread, a Chinese newspaper in lieu of a centre-piece, and on top of the newspaper a dish of fruit. Chairs accompanied the table but they were not what we call dining-room chairs. There was a side table at which we sat, sipped tea, ate fruit and peanuts, and cracked dried watermelon seeds which are always served with tea. The dried watermelon seeds are very popular. They are as much like nothing as anything can be, and to crack them, one runs the risk of breaking a tooth, but they serve an important purpose: they fill in embarrassing moments; where we would poke the fire, or fiddle with a watch-chain; where the Japanese would rearrange the charcoal in the hibachi; there, the Chinese crack watermelon seeds.

A wardrobe with a large mirror occupied a prominent place, while in a place less conspicuous was a washstand with all the toilet articles. You wonder how they could possibly think a washstand suitable for a dining-room; well, it is in this way—after every meal, cloths wrung out of boiling water are passed around upon which the face and hands are wiped, thus making a washstand quite correct for a dining-room; then, as this wiping removes the paint from the ladies' faces, the mirror in the wardrobe is needed to see that it is properly renewed. The real Chinese way, which I saw done in another house, is for the slave to bring a box to the table that looks as if it were a jewel box but which contains paint and powder, brushes and puff, and in the uplifted lid is a mirror. In this foreign room, tea was served in foreign cups that equalled the room in commonness; they were the Sunday-school festival kind. The entire room and its contents were out of harmony with the magnificent Oriental house.

I asked one of the ladies of this home if she would give me a pair of her shoes. She had "golden lilies." She regretted she did not have a new pair and could not understand why I should prefer one showing evidence of wear. They are four and a half inches long, so are not considered very small. In the flip of one, a "cash" piece for luck. These small shoes will in time be curiosities in China, so rapidly is the anti-foot-binding movement spreading.

In one short afternoon call, all the details of such a home could not be grasped; I regretted I had not a thousand eyes and a brain of like capacity. We retraced our steps through those beautiful Oriental rooms and sunny courtyards until we came to the reception-hall where our sedan chairs were; and there, we slipped the first and second fingers of our right hand up our left coat-sleeve, allowing the thumb, third and little finger to rest on the outside of the sleeve as we slowly moved our arms up and down from the elbow only and thus made our adieu before backing into the sedan chairs. The Chinese shake hands, not with each other but each with himself. A man places his right hand over his left so that the two thumbs are parallel to the body and then shakes them slightly, about as much as a violent trembling. One day, I forgot and made a man's handshake, which naturally amused the Chinese.

When we were comfortably seated in our chairs, the bearers hoisted each chair, with a lurch to one side then to the other and with much creaking of bamboo, upon their shoulders, and we jellied out even as we had jellied in. The small boy remembered to say, "Goodbye, come back again," and those were the last words we heard as the unpretentious gate closed and we were once more on those narrow, sunless streets.

When I returned to my residence, I studied the gift of little shoes I had been given and thought about this hateful custom.

What is a bound foot like? Place the thumb on the table, then curl the fingers underneath and you have some idea what the position of the bound foot is—the big toe taking the place of the thumb, and the little toes the fingers—the part of the foot corresponding to the palm of the hand is a very tender place and very susceptible to decay, or gangrene, and must be kept very clean. The foot is humped so that only the big toe and the heel really go into the shoe. This hump is much admired and is called the "Golden Hook."

I did not see a bound foot uncovered. I might have, but shrank from the painful sight, as photographs and description gave one a fair idea of this barbarous custom inflicting life-long suffering on millions, no matter how gradually and carefully it is performed.

The crowding of all the toes under the foot, save the big toe, the arching of the foot, the gradual snapping of the instep, all cause a life of misery from about the age of seven. This is when the binding is carefully done: what if it be carelessly done? In that case, the feet often rot, blood poisoning sets in, and death becomes a happy release. I have this information not from such as hastily travel through a few of the ports, or from the uninformed people, but from those who love the Chinese and have been with them for years.

One day, I was talking about the Emperor to an old lady, who, at the age of 70, had gone through the painful process of unbinding her feet two years before I met her. She went away to her room and returned with a picture of the Emperor. My friends remonstrated with her for walking so far, but she said, "Now I do not mind going many times to my room from here; but before I unbound my feet to walk from my room to here (*here* was the main reception-hall of the house) was Hell." My friend, knowing the Chinese ladies so well, was ever mindful when calling in their homes not to keep them standing, for that would cause the feet to bleed. This custom is so well known to outsiders that there is no need to go farther into the subject except to say, "Do not believe anything you may hear about it not paining them." The nation is awakening to the cruelty of this, and anti-foot-binding societies are now in the leading cities. The membership of these societies is purely Chinese, although their beginnings can be credited to foreign influence. It will be many, many years, however, before women will cease to totter painfully on their big toe and heel.

I am, of course, no advocate of foot-binding, but I confess that the tiny red shoes, exquisitely embroidered, peeping from under the short skirts of a Chinese lady, look very dainty and attractive. I can quite understand the men admiring the small foot when they do not have to suffer for it.

These small shoes that were given me are reposing on my

drawing-room table, yet I have criticized a washstand in a dining-room!

Chapter Nine

Wherein foreign influences are remarked upon, modes of dress are further studied, and the President of the Anti-Foot-Binding Society is visited.

Our next call was on a Chinese lady of high class, now in reduced circumstances. This home seemed small indeed after the Mohammedan one of 300 rooms, but my friend and I were welcome and that in any country counts for more than a mere display of opulence, although wealth and welcome combined may be ideal. The reception-hall in which we were received was very near the front gate but the great array of ancestral tablets told a story not in keeping with the humbleness of the home. A Chinese young lady who had been educated in the United States was there giving lessons in English to the sons of the house. In Chinese estimation a teacher ranks high, and every respect is shown. So when we were seated in our proper places at the square polished table upon which were peanuts, selections of oranges, candy and dried watermelon seeds for our refreshment, the hostess offered the remaining seat at the table to the teacher. She of course declined the honour with proper humility; thereupon the hostess urged her again and again, even to the extent of catching hold of her and trying to force her onto the chair. By this time, it sounded to me as if they were scrapping so I interfered, in the bold way foreigners have and are forgiven because they are barbarians, and motioned to the hostess to take the seat at the table, and to the teacher to sit near me so that we could speak in English. Preliminaries being over, tea in those double cups was served.

The boys in this home wore foreign boots of coarse leather and of a very homely make, but they were as proud of them as a young white boy is of his first pair of trousers.

In spite of the American boycott, which was helping to make Soochow a dangerous place for white people to live, there was much display in many shops of foreign pots and pans and other household necessaries, which seemed more than was needed by the 80 white residents of Soochow; so there must be a native demand for things. In the most unexpected places, a touch of foreign would be seen. Many barbers, who went from street to street, into the temple courtyards or along alleys plying their trade, wherever men gathered, had discarded their ancient brass hot water basins for Western blue-and-white enamelled tin ones. I presume style exists even in matters tonsorial.

We are fond of sighing for a land where fashions do not change; and we think this is so in China and Japan, but that is only another of the many mistakes we make concerning the Far East. Dame Fashion, although called by another name in the Orient, is the same firm, cruel despot here as where you are. Western women are pulled tight in corsets; Eastern women bind their feet, as mentioned earlier, and bind also their bosoms. A band is tightened across the breasts to produce a flat appearance that is highly beautiful in their eyes. I am told this causes great pain; but it being a mark of beauty, women will suffer and smile. Pictures we have seen with Chinese ladies wearing loose-fitting coats with wide sleeves, are not up to date. Today, fashionable Chinese ladies, and there are many of them, wear their coats very tight and to get the proper effect, round the body underneath the coat is a broad band, fastened up the back with horn buttons. This band being without shape is exceeding uncomfortable to the wearer and makes stooping an impossibility, but as there are always slaves at hand this does not matter. Now, the sleeves of the coat itself are tight—plain and short, coming to about three inches above the wrist. This garment is fur-lined for the winter and as the sleeves are not cut separately and then sewn in, but cut with the coat and thus fit perfectly only when the arms are outstretched like a sign-post, they hang with a hump at the shoulder blade that is like a deformity. But such is fashion!

The women around Soochow and Shanghai wear skirts; position, rank and many things are shown by the skirt. For example, a widow can never wear a red one, unless, in some parts, she has a son married, although she may wear certain other colours; little wives can never wear any but a black skirt; girls never wear any skirt, but wear gaily coloured trousers reaching to the ankle and a shirt-like garment covering the upper part of the body. I never ceased being amused at the schoolgirls whenever they sat down, for they always, unconsciously, tilted up the little tails of their upper garment so that they would not be crushed. When a girl becomes a young lady her long abundant braid of black hair that heretofore hung down like a pigtail and had been fastened with coloured yarn is coiled over one ear and gaily ornamented; then the next stage is to have the hair coiled in all its glossiness at the back of the head—very low down just now—and then she may don a skirt. A Chinese girl wears her front hair in a fringe. This is a real native fashion, and at present the correct thing is to have it cut in a semi-circle around the face and curled.

From the time a girl is quite young, if she belongs to a rich family, the father gives her jewels—chiefly pearls and jade—so that every lady has a beautiful collection of them. The principal way to display jewels is on their head-dress, which is only worn in winter—hence great ceremonial feasts are held then. The cap consists of two pear-shaped pieces of black cloth fastened so that the broad pieces come over the ears and the narrow part, which is about two inches wide, above the forehead. On this narrow piece in a straight line above the nose, are always two large jewels, usually immense pearls, while the rest of the cap is thickly covered with pearls and jade, and fastened to the cap somewhere over the ear is an ornament made of pearls and shaped something like a hand, the fingers projecting toward the face. When these elaborate ornaments are worn, quick movements of the head are out of the question. In fact the whole dress of a Chinese lady, from the pearl-bedecked head to the bound feet, necessitates a stiff manner, reminding one of marionettes. The tiny shoes also indicate the rank and position of the wearers and there are fashions in shoes as in other things. The pair the Moham-medan lady gave me were of red brocade silk upon which unnatural looking butterflies are embroidered. The butter-fly—an emblem of freedom—what a farce! This red founda-tion is finished at the top of the shoe by a piping of royal blue brocade, which is followed around by bands of green, black and gold braid; in the tab at the back is a lucky coin; a white cotton sock is worn.

In Soochow there is a school for Chinese girls run entirely by the Chinese at which in 1905 there were 88 girls. The limit was placed at bound feet; none with bound feet was eligible for admittance. If the feet be bound when the scholar comes then the unbinding process must begin. Although this school is a mere atom in China, still it means much, for Soochow is a leading city, and what the leader does others will do. The Chi-nese are, in everything they can, copying the Japanese. Calis-thenics are taught, and the little girls are dressed in uniforms similar to those of Japanese soldiers; a funnier sight could not be seen anywhere. In one purely Chinese school I heard that the way they gave music lessons was for one to take the lesson, with the others looking on. Even in the four weeks that I was in China I heard of so many purely Chinese reforms, suggested of course by Western civilization, that it is easily seen that China's awakening has come. Will the darkest hours be before the dawn? Will the present disturbances be worse than the Boxer trouble?

I was taken to call upon a Chinese lady who is president of the Anti-Foot-Binding Society in Soochow, and so influential that the foreigners call her the Empress-Dowager. Her home had been built for 300 years and it looked its age. Time had not dealt kindly with it; instead of picturesque ruins there were only unsightly signs of decay, while the skeleton of a sedan chair that rested, thickly coated with dust, in an entrance hall, gave an uncanny feeling. This lady was most advanced in her views; she had educated all her family except one daughter who, she said, was engaged to be married and she did not intend to educate her. This is not "advanced" in the technical sense, and it shows that even the advanced ones are still weighed down by custom.

As we were seated at tea in the old reception-hall with its stone floor, its lofty domed roof with the great rafters showing, its window-doors of oyster shell and wooden lattice work, its tables polished with the grease of many meals, and while our hostess discoursed on the anti-foot-binding movement, higher education or on the doings of the court at Peking (for her husband when living, had been a court-official), hens meandered over the floor picking up such crumbs as might fall and adding an occasional "cluck-cluck" to the general conversation. A servant rudely interrupted her mistress to ask if something cooking was nearly done. A cat enjoyed the contents of a bowl that were for another purpose than her pleasure. With cupboard doors opened showing a disorderly array of utensils, and with clutter everywhere and things in full view that we usually keep out of sight of company, I was reminded

89

of Dickens' Mrs. Jellaby in a Chinese setting.

Now bear in mind that this was a nice Chinese home and any Chinese girl who married into it would be considered very lucky indeed.

In China marriage is for the family, not for the individual. The aim of a Chinese in marriage is to continue his family name, have descendants for ancestral worship, and to give to his mother a daughter-in-law for a servant. The wishes of the contracting parties are not consulted, and usually they never see each other until after they are married. The marriage is arranged by the parents through a go-between. The position of a go-between is most remunerative.

Chapter Ten

In which Margaret is impressed by the solemnity and style of a non-Christian wedding of quality, learns that a green chair is superior to a red one and offers the reader recipes for steamed shark's fins and bird's nest soup.

While in Soochow, I was fortunate in being invited to an aristocratic heathen Chinese wedding. (The wedding I had attended earlier, in Shanghai, had been a Chinese-Christian ceremony.) The invitation is worthy of a description. Red being the wedding colour, the invitation was in three shades of red. The envelope was a terra-cotta with a strip of bright pinkish-red pasted on, upon which the name of the guest was written in the usual Chinese style and characters. The envelope was not sealed, and inside was a large piece of bright red paper folded in a peculiar way with a printed picture of two men on the outside fold. There is a legend connected with these men, but all I know is that they are called two friends, and always figure at weddings.* This bright red paper was merely the wrapper for the invitation proper, which was written in black ink on pinkish-red paper. In the right hand column, reading from top to bottom, were the names of those to be married and of those who sent the invitation. In the next column to the left at the top was "your presence will give light" (a dainty piece of flattery, which I did not expect from the Chinese, who are not renowned for flowery speeches). In the third and last column, about the middle, were the words for "do not refuse.' I did not refuse.

The wedding of which I am speaking took place in Soochow in December, 1905. Even if one were to witness a dozen weddings, it would be difficult to grasp all the details, and fashion differs with years and in different places; the essential ceremony, however, is probably the same.

Ordinarily, a bride comes to the home of her future husband's family in a sedan-chair covered with red satin heavily embroidered and bejewelled with imitation jewels and bedecked with tinsel and small mirrors; gaily coloured lanterns hang from the chair, which is preceded by a band, and outrunners, dressed in red and wearing conically shaped hats. The bridegroom's family and guests are notified that the bride is coming by fireworks and the sounds of the music and the shouting of outrunners—these three combined make an alarming noise to the unused Westerner. They sent remembrances of Boxer Riots through my mind, but when my friend whispered, "The bride is coming," I forgot all such unpleasant things in the excitement of seeing the bride enter.

She came in a plain green chair with a red rag tied to the top-knot. My friend, who had attended many weddings, had never seen a green chair used before and could not understand the meaning. It appeared to be an insult. The groom's people send the chair, and perhaps they thought the bride's family so inferior that a grand red chair was not necessary? Was it, that as this family were progressive, they were endeavouring to cut down the great expenses connected with Chinese weddings? Was it that they were stingy? Why? Inquiry, made later on, revealed the fact that anyone could use a red chair who could pay for it, but only those of a certain rank could use a green chair—green being the official colour for a chair—so these people were aristocratic enough to use a green chair.

The bride apparently came too soon; so her chair, herself within it, was set aside until the proper moment arrived. Dirty, rude street people crowded in and pushed the guests into the background; in fact, they wandered all over the house, and the people of the house seemed pleased to have them do so. Hurried preparations were made; red carpet spread on the stone floor; tall red candles with a dragon design on the sides were lit and so was the incense. I peered around for the ancestral tablets, but could not see them, so my friend, who could speak Chinese, asked where they were and two red lacquered boxes high on the rafter against the domed roof were pointed out as containing the tablets. Very often when the occupants own the house the tablets are placed up there—very difficult to reach in case of fire, I should think.

Underneath these tablets was a table upon which food and wine, an offering to the spirits of the departed, was placed. At last, the auspicious moment arrived; the bride's chair was brought into a prominent position and she was asked to come out by a master-of-ceremonies, whom I, in my ignorance, had mistaken for one of the street people. The invitation was given in a high theatrical tone that was, no doubt, supposed to be very alluring, but the bride did not come because custom demanded that she shall delay as long as possible. At last, she left her chair but left it slowly and with the assistance of the professional managers. These professional managers are a fine institution for they are not excited, not being personally interested, and take all the responsibility for the arrangements.

The bride came forth with a large square of red satin completely enveloping her. I said how hot that would be on a

summer day, but was told that the Chinese did not have weddings in hot weather for many reasons, principally because December was the lucky month (just as we say June is) and because the winter dress of the ladies, and doubtless of the man, is much handsomer than the summer one.

The real ceremony began with the groom leading the bride by a red rag to the centre of the great reception-hall that opens out upon the courtyard, and here they worshipped Heaven and Earth by prostrations toward the outside; then turned and worshipped in the same manner at the ancestral tablets that were fastened to the roof. As it was quite impossible for the bride to prostrate herself, her will had to be taken for the deed.

Meanwhile the family had assembled on the red carpet in rows, each generation in a row. In the first row were a grandmother of the groom and his great aunt, and in the last row was a baby about six months old; the rows between were, of course, well filled. There was no priest for the service, but all the necessary talking was done by a master-of-ceremonies. He said something, thereupon the entire family of about 80 people prostrated themselves and then arose, all except the old grandmother; the frequent prostrations and risings being too much for one of her years she remained prostrated until the end and then was assisted in rising by a little slave girl.

This ancestral worship, with prostrations for each ancestor, or perhaps each generation of ancestors, was intensely interesting. The ritual was shouted by the master-of-ceremonies in a strained voice and in a language unknown to most of those present (ancient classic language). My impression is that there was a silence everywhere during the ceremony of ancestral worship, but this impression may only have been left because of the solemnity of the occasion. It was very solemn. There was a short ceremony in connection with the food set for the ancestral spirits. The setting of food for the spirits made them seem very near, and gave me the uncomfortable feeling that they were not happy because of the need for these temporal things.

The ancestral worship was followed by the bridal couple paying their respects to the groom's family beginning with the grandmother who sat in a red covered chair while the young groom prostrated himself, and his bride did the best she could, which was to slowly move her arms up and down. The groom's mother insisted that my friend, whom she wished to honour, should sit in the chair and receive respect. Now, it would have been very rude for my friend to have done so; she would probably never be asked to the house again, yet her hostess caught her by the arm and someone else pushed her and someone pulled and she was nearly forced into the chair. There was an undignified struggle, the only undignified part in the whole affair. Everybody knew my friend would not sit down, at least ought not to, and there was no intention that she should, yet she was nearly compelled to; such is Chinese etiquette.

The marriage was over. The bride was led by the groom with a red rag and was escorted by tall lighted candles, through a narrow passage and up a steep stair to her room, which after that night she would not leave for one month and then only to pay a visit to her mother. In this room the bridal couple sat on the edge of one of those much-bedecked Chinese beds. I wish I could remember all the things that are put in and on the bridal-bed but I cannot remember anything but one talisman that guarded against quarrels in marriage. There was such a succession of things, the like of which I had never seen before, that it was impossible to see, let alone remember everything and its meaning.

All this time the bride was enshrouded in the red satin veil but now a bar was taken from the bridal-bed and the bride's mother-in-law stood in front of the bride but with her back to her and, with the assistance of the ever-present managers, the red satin veil was removed to the bar, which the mother-in-law held over her shoulder. This symbolized the mother-in-law's sovereignty. Food was brought and offered to the bride and groom but they only tasted it though they must both have been hungry. We were asked to leave the room as the bride was to change her marriage hat for one suitable for the feast, which was to follow.

We had been in that room earlier in the day while awaiting the arrival of the bride. There, we sipped tea out of those hard-to-manipulate cups, cracked watermelon seeds and ate rose candy, like our gumdrops flavoured with real rose leaf, the roses being grown outside the city wall; it was delicious.

Into one wall was built a cupboard with foreign glass windows; it was for curios and among the valuables was a medal bearing Prince Albert's head. Seeing it, I exclaimed, and the man who was head of the house opened the case and with pride showed it to me. It was to commemorate the opening of the Crystal Palace. I rose in their estimation when I said the

Prince Consort was my King; which was not strictly true, but how else could I explain? Many were the surprises in China; but seeing the Prince Consort's Crystal Palace medal in an interior city 2200 years old was one of the greatest. The Chinese minister in London at that time was a friend of these people and he had brought this home for them.

While the bride was changing her head-gear, servants and slaves were preparing tables for the bride's feast. Only highly honoured guests sat at this feast—it was indeed an honorary affair, for no-one ate. The groom's mother stood in the centre of the reception-hall, and a professional female manager brought her to each guest in turn to whom she bowed in Chinese fashion as I described earlier, as if shaking hands with herself, then returned to the centre of the room and stood there until the female manager went to the guest who had been bowed to and led her to the centre of the room facing the groom's mother. Thereupon the guest bowed in the same Chinese fashion (even I did it as gracefully as I could), then the manager brought a metal wine cup and metal chopsticks and conducted the hostess and guest to the guest's seat at the table. When all were seated who were privileged to, the bride's feast began by these managers offering food and wine to the bride and groom, neither of whom partook, nor did the guests. When the bride and groom arose from this feast, they went away to call at the house of the bride's people. This is usually done the day after the wedding, but for some reason these aristocratic people crowded everything into one day.

After the bridal party left, the guests sipped tea, ate sweets and cracked watermelon seeds until the feast arrived. First came shark's fins and crabs, and then bird's nest soup, and if anyone desires to make these dishes I give the recipes.

Shark's Fins: "The manner of washing sun-dried shark's fins is: first, take the fins and place in a cooking-pan, add wood-ashes and boil in several waters. Then take out and scrape away the roughness of the fins. If not clean, boil again, and scrape again until properly cleaned, then change the water and boil again. Take out, cut away the flesh, and keep only the fins. Then boil once again. Put in spring water. Be careful in changing water and soak them thoroughly for it is necessary that the lime taste be taken from them. Then put the fins into the soup, stew three times till tender. Serve in a bowl placing crab-meat below them, and add a little ham on top." "Delicious" is the word. It is indeed delicious. Never having cooked them, I cannot guarantee this recipe, but give it as the only one I have.

Bird's Nest Soup: this is a luxury made of dried saliva from certain birds' nests found in caves on the seashore. The bird is native of Malaya and Ceylon. The nests are gathered at considerable risk, and the best quality commands a high price. Chinese consider it stimulating and strengthening and it forms, with shark's fins, the first dish at grand dinners.

"Take white clean bird's nests and soak thoroughly. Pick out all feathers. Boil nests in soup or water until tender and of the colour of jadestone. Place pigeon's eggs below, and add some hamshreds on top. Boil again slowly with a little fluid. If required sweet, then boil in clear water until tender, add sugar and then eat.

I can say that bird's nest soup is not only decorative on the menu but is very palatable. I am particularly fond of shark's fins as well.

Another delicious dish, from a Chinese standpoint, is eggs a hundred days old. I had no opportunity of tasting this delicacy; otherwise, I would have shut my eyes and tried it. It is not so bad as the description would make one think, for the egg is put into a pickle of some kind until aged, or seasoned, when it becomes the ideal of the fastidious Celestial gourmet.

* Invitations often had two people bowing as if welcoming guests; or a character representing double happiness; or a dragon and a phoenix.

Chapter Eleven

An occasion of consequence finds Margaret attending a ten-course birthday feast while red banners flutter and musicians and jugglers perform.

My last glimpse of family life in Soochow was at a birthday feast in a household of 125 persons. There were no men present, nor any Chinese guests, for the Chinese ladies have almost no social intercourse, but there were head wives, little wives, children, servants and women slaves (there may be men slaves in China but I did not see any, to know them as such, nor did I hear of them). Surprisingly, the guest of honour whose birthday it was was not present. She never put in an appearance, much to the relief of the other ladies of the household, for she was said to be a Tartar. As it was, the ladies took turns going and playing chess with her. This home was the most refined one I visited in Soochow. The ladies had none of the boisterous manner, and did none of that loud talking in coarse tones that is so common among Chinese ladies, and which grates on the ear of one accustomed to the gentleness and delicacy of vocal sound of the Japanese ladies. Indeed, these ladies at this birthday feast would be ladies anywhere in the world.

We started for this house in a boat; but as the boat became wedged in the narrow canal, and moving would take perhaps an hour, we landed and walked the short distance that lay between our stranded boat and the house.

In the courtyard was stationed a band, the best in this leading literary and artistic city. It was good; I am sure it was good from the sounds, but they were strange to the foreign ear and could not be appreciated as they ought; it was very different from the noise that one heard in the streets and that one thinks of when a Chinese band is mentioned. This music was in minor keys, and weird and soft. The performers were all men and sang a dialogue in voices keyed so high as to be extremely feminine, thereby showing their vocal skill. The training to accomplish this is severe, and must be begun when they are small boys. They made a most typical Oriental picture as they sat in the open around what, for want of a better description, I will call a table.

This table was about 6 feet by 3 feet and upon it was a pot of tea, perhaps hot wine; whatever it was, it was in great demand. Above the table was a framework about six feet in height of much-decorated and much-carved wood, interset with glass of various hues, and the pictures on the glass were shown to advantage by lanterns hung from every available place on this framework.

The guests sat in the reception-hall as they listened to the music. In this hall was the family altar, trimmed with emblems suitable to the occasion. The colour scheme was red. Large satin banners with characters in gilt, wishing long life and happiness, hung upon the walls. In the place of honour was a wall-hanging representing the Goddess of Mercy riding on a goose's back and coming down from Heaven to Earth to attend a birthday feast, which was going on in the lower corner of the picture. Surely here is the origin of our Mother Goose rhymes. My friend said that the Chinese had many nursery rhymes similar to ours. I called the bird a goose; it might have been a stork* and had something to do with the German legend of the stork.

On the altar, leaning against this picture, was a tablet covered with red paper upon which there was much writing and that was the tablet of the one honoured by the feast. In front of this tablet were displayed the presents, which were of food daintily garnished, while in front of the presents stood two large pewter candlesticks with tall red candles burning, and between them was the incense urn. The incense for this occasion was in the shape of a character for good luck that looked exactly as our fireworks do in the daytime; but instead of going off with great display, only smouldered and emitted a sweet heavy odour.

Once while I was listening intently to the music and trying to make head or tail out of it, I was touched on the shoulder by one of the ladies so that my attention would be drawn to a ceremony that was going on. A red satin cushion had been laid on the stone floor in front of the altar and the eldest and youngest grandson were making their obeisance to—just what, I am not sure, but I think to the red tablet that represented the honoured person, because after the obeisances, it was taken by the eldest grandson, followed by the youngest, outside into the street and there burnt.

At this stage of the proceedings, an imitation dragon of fearful appearance was to come amongst us and strike terror, but as the feast was almost ready, this thrilling experience, what the children were eager for, was delayed.

We were ushered into another reception-room and there served with tea in which rose leaves had been put, peanuts, Chinese candy and dried watermelon seeds, and for something extra, pieces of Japanese pears. The head lady took a handful of the eatables and put them on the table in front of her guests. From this room, we were taken up into the show bedrooms of the house. The bedrooms, in all the houses I was in, had wooden floors painted a dark red, but no carpets or rugs.

On a shelf of beautiful native wood, covered with a common foreign cloth for style, were some curios that we admired as we sipped tea and talked on various subjects of interest— dress being one. It is so nice that women the world over can have subjects of mutual interest.

On this occasion, I learned that clothes cannot be put on to

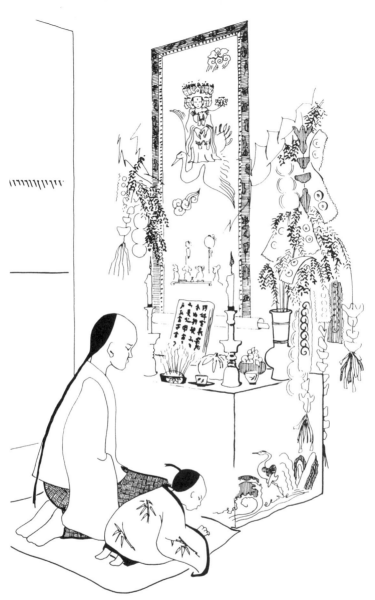

suit the climate or the temperature of the wearer but must be
donned on the arrival of a certain date, set, I think, by the

Imperial Court. Who sets the fashion in China? Tailors, not by the name of Worth, though, but whose decrees are followed as blindly by the Chinese as Worth's are by Europeans.

Foreigners think these distinctions in Eastern dress much fuss about nothing, forgetting that they have similar distinction, the breach of which appears to them as ludicrous or shocking. Imagine a widow in a pale pink dress or a child in a black basque. Is it not sometimes said of a woman of perhaps 50 years that she dresses like a young girl? It is when one comes to the East and sees Orientals wearing Occidental dress that one realizes our life is more than surrounded; it is filled to the centre with etiquette and fastidious form.

A lady told me that when she came out from Europe by the Suez in 1905, a Chinaman on board the steamer always dressed for dinner, dress-coat and vest, tie, and showed an expanse of white shirt front, and when seen sitting at the table, he was *de rigueur,* but when he stood up, his mauve silk Chinese trousers more than suggested the ludicrous. There are a few foreigners who wear Chinese dress, mostly the members of the China Inland Mission, and I am told that at times they make very funny mistakes in matters of detail. To see a fair-haired foreigner wearing the front of his head shaved and a long fair queue hanging down his back is as funny a sight as any Chinese combination of our dress could be.

Our talk of dress was interrupted and we were reminded of the birthday feast awaiting us in the dining-room. I was motioned to take a certain seat at the table, and as it is polite in my country to conform to direction in such case, I bowed and took it, then there was a fluttering among the head ladies of the house for I had been, by mistake, bidden to take a humble seat with my back to the heavens (as seen through an open door). This would never do so I was changed and sat facing outside, and when all the guests, six in number, were seated at the three sides of the table, the two head wives sat at the fourth. How there came to be two head ladies of equal rank my friend could never fathom; but there they were and they shared the honours.

At each place on the polished white table were a pair of ivory chopsticks and a porcelain spoon. There was no table-cloth, no napkins, no pepper and salt, no confusing array of knives, forks and spoons. No, just a dainty pair of ivory chop-sticks, which are the most difficult of all chopsticks to use, and the spoon; and what cannot be done at the table with these is considered work for the kitchen. Although we had already sipped tea and partaken of sweets many times, still it had to be done once more, for they were the first course of the actual meal. So we sipped tea and cracked watermelon seeds and waited for the second course, which we knew would be some-thing we were all very fond of, namely, shark's fins. The dishes are not removed from the table every time fresh ones come on, so soon the table is crowded and only those dishes that have been longest on the table are moved to make way for the new ones.

I do not remember the order of the ten or twelve courses but generally speaking, they grade from the most expensive—shark's fins and bird's nest soup—to the cheapest—rice. (The

Chinese rice is much inferior to the Japanese, indeed many of the poor Japanese sell their home-grown rice and buy that from China and make a profit on the transaction. The Chinese serve their food very hot; many of the bowls have double bottoms and hot water is put in the lower part.) Somewhere between the first and last course comes a dish of sea-slugs. I did not relish them although I confess it was mostly due to imagination because of the name and of the helpless way a fat slug would hang over the chopstick when it was lifted from its bed of soup.

How delicious are the Chinese soups! I like almost all Chinese food, finding it very like our own, but I object strongly to the way it is served. Everyone dips his spoon into the public soup bowl and then his chopsticks into the same bowl in search of a piece of meat. My hostess, wishing to serve me with some more fish, wiped her chopsticks in her mouth, then put them into the fish bowl and laid an especially good piece of fish on my spoon for me to eat. One does many unusual things in the East.

The Chinese ladies were pleased that I could use chopsticks, as I had only been a few weeks in their country. Even little babies learn to use them; in a surprisingly short time, the baby fingers become very skilful.

The feast ended by the washing of faces and hands on a towel wrung out of boiling water (this cloth was frequently too hot for me to hold) and when we went into the outer reception-hall to hear the music, the higher servants, who were feasting at a table placed in front of the altar, moved to our deserted table, and servants of a lower order took their places in the outer hall. The head servant in this house ruled the ladies with a rod of iron. Servants in a Chinese home are all-powerful as they are also spies on their mistresses, and much grief comes from their malicious tale-bearing. You ask, "But what do the lower servants—the slaves—do?" Slaves seem to be personal attendants of the ladies. After the feast, the head ladies were listening to the music when a slave came up to one of them with a water-pipe filled with tobacco and thrust it into her mouth. The lady never made any sign of knowing that the pipe was between her lips except to take a puff—only one whiff, for then the pipe was exhausted and the slave withdrew it and replenished it to stick in another lady's mouth. I thought the Japanese pipe queer enough with its two whiffs of tobacco, but it is small and two whiffs are its complement. The Chinese pipe is stranger still for, although a big affair of several compartments and a cord and tassel, it holds only one whiff.

In an outer room, a juggler showed his skill. He was said to be the best in Soochow, but I have observed that the finest jugglers and acrobats go abroad, where money is to be had.

The band was playing in the courtyard and beyond was the old entrance gate, strong enough to keep out an army. Around were the high grey walls of the courtyard and above was the blue of the heavens, filled with stars that twinkled softly down upon this bizarre scene. Ere we left at 9.30 PM, a big moon came slowly over the top of the great courtyard wall. What more could one want?

We were invited to return the next day to see theatricals by the leading professionals in this centre of the Celestial Empire. I regretted that I had to miss seeing something of the Chinese stage, but the unsettled state of the country made it necessary for me to return to Shanghai. A foreign gentleman who could speak Chinese was going down the next day and it was thought advisable that I should go with him.

* Probably the crane, which is associated with longevity in Chinese folklore.

Chapter Twelve

In which Margaret rides through a menacing mob in a jinrikisha; there are forebodings about China's future and final reflections during a train journey as her tale draws to a close.

Sorry as I was to miss the theatricals in Soochow, I am glad to have been in Shanghai for the riots on 18 December, 1905. At the time of the riots, many of the prominent Chinese who had daughters at the mission school left them there, for they considered their daughters safer in the school than in their homes; one father who came for his daughters at the beginning of the Christmas holidays, which was also the end of the dangerous time of the riots, said he felt that they were most secure in the school. He said he had been mobbed on the street, with bricks and mud, because he wore foreign clothes. When asked if he fought, he replied, "Oh no, I thought it best to be 'wise as a serpent and harmless as a dove' and besides, what was the use of 'kicking against the bricks.'"

I acted upon the same principle when I was caught downtown in the mob that was stoning the German Vice-Consul. It seemed incredible that the people on Nanking Road, who only some fifteen minutes before appeared to be out for a holiday with no unkind look or word for me, were now ready to kill every foreigner on whom they could lay their hands. A foreign gentleman accosted me with, "You ought not to be here. Go home."

That was no news to me, I knew it only too well.

"Then I must get to the other end of Nanking Road," I said.

"You cannot," he glowered. A lifetime experience of brothers has taught me that such a tone of voice is useless to resist.

"What shall I do?" I asked meekly in the humblest tone imaginable, as if I were a clinging creature ever dependent on the lords of creation.

He took me to the Central Hotel and left me with orders to stay there until the soldiers were summoned.

Not having him nor anyone else to cling to, I became my natural self and acted. First, I tried to get my friends over the telephone, but could not; then I rang an acquaintance and said, "Send your carriage for me, I am stranded at the Central Hotel."

The answer came: "I can't. *Mafoo* has struck."

"Send your servants for me."

"I can't, they are terrified to go out-of-doors."

This frightened me for the first time; and although the hotel was a foreign one, I could not see any people but Chinese. Looking out on the Bund, which was swarming with evil-faced men who seemed to be everywhere, I realized that my only chance of reaching the British Consulate lay in going immediately before the news came that the rioting had become general.

Hailing a *jinrikisha* (I was fortunate in getting a man to pull me for they were inclined to refuse foreigners), I hurried to the British Consulate. A Chinese mob is a bright blue mob and a cruel, cowardly mob. Not understanding a word of what was being said gave me a feeling of terrible helplessness and I was thankful indeed when I bowled into the British Consulate compound. As I was the first to arrive there with the news of the mobbing, they looked at me in a way that plainly said, "You silly creature; how like a woman!" This made me angry and I thereupon frankly confessed to being frightened and to coming there for protection. Half an hour later, they thought differently for then they had marines and gatling-guns in their compound.

A gentleman there offered to escort me to my friends, and

although he was quite sure I was making a fuss about nothing he took the precaution of getting a very heavy walking-stick. We started. The side street was quiet. This annoyed me for I feared I must seem a "silly creature; how like a woman!" but when we turned on to Hankow Road, the men were so many that the street looked as if it had a bright blue carpet, the yellow faces were as the pattern. At the sight of them, my spirits rose in spite of my fear for I have a horror of being thought silly.

When riding in *jinrikishas,* it is necessary to go single file and as my *jinrikisha* was first, I had to keep turning around to see if my escort were following, for not having any idea who he was how did I know he would remain faithful? We were forced to go slowly through this evil-looking mob whose glances were threatening and whose words—it was easy to see—were not complimentary. My escort called to me, and looking around, I found that the mob was holding his ricksha. I did not know that at that very moment only three blocks away a man six feet three inches in height and strong in proportion was being dragged from his ricksha and abused and that violence, in general, was being done; they let my escort's 'ricksha go, and he called to me, "Don't be frightened." Thereupon I cheerfully replied, "I am not frightened when you are with me." This sounded very heroic but had anyone said another sympathetic word to me, I would have burst out crying, so great was the nervous tension.

We passed the eastern gate of the school compound and stopped at the western, or residence gate, which was locked. It seemed a long time before it was opened, probably less than minute, but when one is on the wrong side of the fence a minute is a long, long time. No sooner had I entered the western gate than outside of the eastern gate, there was terrific firing, and as we knew not whether it was by the marines nor by the mob, times were exciting. Fortunately for us, it was by the marines and unfortunately for one poor Chinaman, who was killed. He lay outside of our compound for the rest of the day. In all, during this riot, 60 Chinese were killed and the pity of it was that many were only innocent onlookers. No foreigners were seriously injured. The foreign women in the suburbs all fled to the country club where military protection was afforded. During the excitement there were many tales of cruelty to foreigners who were unconscious of it, and tales of incendiarism that afterwards could not be verified. The mob lacked a leader, method and quickness of action, to carry out its schemes.

It is well known by people of other nationalities what inordinate boasters the citizens of the United States are, so there was considerable interchanging of smiles and nudging of elbows when the riot broke out and they did not have a warship anywhere near, although they had as much warning as the other nations who were ready to send men ashore as soon as word reached them. The riot was on a Monday morning

and the first United States warship arrived on the following Friday. One enthusiastic citizen of that country remarked upon hearing that their belated warship had at last arrived; "Oh! I am so thankful our warship has arrived." That is all right, everyone has a right to be thankful to see their own warship in times of danger, but what about the next remark? "I feel so safe now that our soldiers are here." Politeness forbade me making any direct reference to this, but I took the occasion to say that the week had seemed very long since the riot began; instead of the fifth day, it seemed more like the fifteenth day.

Great changes are taking place in China. "Young China" dons Western clothes, wearing Western trousers of a cut that I never thought would occur to anyone. He discards the queue, and thinks he knows more than the older men of his country, which, however, is not exclusively an Oriental trait. He may, but he goes about in a wrong way to show it. He only proves the old adage "a little learning is a dangerous thing." He goes abroad and receives a smattering of Western education, principally in a country where the trend of education is to exalt the youth of the country at the expense of the mature, and returns "cocky" (that word is most descriptive); or else learns of the heroes of the world and of what they have done for their respective countries, and is puffed up, and longs to be great by one stroke. He sees China's need of reformation but is too impetuous and uninformed to be a leader, able only to incite to riot, damaging himself and his cause.

China is awakening to her situation. We fear the yellow peril. China fears the white peril. A cartoon published in a Chinese paper shows why they fear the white peril. In the north is the Russian bear; in the centre the English bulldog; in the south-east the Yankee eagle; in the south the French frog; while about Formosa is Japan's lasso; and around Shantung are a line of German sausages.

All China is seething and bubbling underneath; the people

want something that they have not but know not what it is, nor how to get it. They are to be pitied; so, too, are the officials, for they can see both sides—see that "young China" is too cocky and "old China" too fossilized, yet can see that they themselves lack the necessary knowledge and power to shape their country's destiny. What China needs is a leader, and history the world over shows that when the time is ripe, a leader will be forthcoming.

They are their own worst enemies, they do not trust themselves. This was clearly shown during the Shanghai riots when the *Taotai,* in his official palanquin and surrounded by his mounted guards was in constant fear that the mob would attack him. He visited the shops on the principal streets and begged the keepers to open and thus restore confidence. This they did, but only while the *Taotai* was present. As soon as he passed on, up went the shutters. That well-meaning official, hearing of this, turned and remonstrated, but the shopkeepers replied, "Your Honour, as long as you are here we are safe, but without your Honour's protection we would be looted." Looted, and by whom? By the foreign devils whom they are endeavouring to chase from their country? No, but by their own kith and kin and by 1500 of their soldiers who were that day disguised as the *leer-mong* and were inciting the people to deeds of violence. The country is filled with robbers and the peaceful people are in terror of them; consequently, isolated houses are never seen. It is said that even the night watchmen are in league with the robbers, for should a person not think it necessary to tip the watchman he is sure to be robbed.

As the riots subsided, my sojourn was coming to an end. My last glimpses were of a calmer China—from the windows of a railway train on the short ride from Shanghai to Neziang.

The railway station at Shanghai is a modern Western building. A Chinese clerk sells the tickets, but a British Sikh policeman guards the gates and punches the tickets, which are printed in English as well as in Chinese. The conductor, in a foreign uniform of strange cut and with a pigtail hanging from beneath his peaked cap, said, "Tickets please." This was a surprise. But that was the end of his knowledge of English. He was a member of the Presbyterian Church.

The train fairly crawled along but it was a pleasure to watch the expressions on the faces of the people; for most of them it was their first ride. Coming back, a foreign gentleman got on whom I knew, and as there was a half seat unoccupied in front of me I motioned for him to sit there, but he did not. I thought if he preferred standing to sitting in front of me and beside a Chinese woman, he could go on standing. Afterwards, I found out that he knew it would be insulting to the Chinese woman to sit beside her.

I had heard of the graves of China but never realized what that meant until on this railway trip. Graves were everywhere. The whole country was simply a graveyard. The small spaces where there were neither tombs nor coffins standing were vegetable gardens.

Some of the tombs are earth mounds now grass-covered, others are small houses built of brick with holes in each end through which the spirits come and go at will. This is very necessary, for a Chinaman on the train gravely told us that each person had three spirits when living and 600 when dead. These openings for the 600 spirits were quite small and I longed to ask how much room a spirit took—if the 600 could go through the small opening abreast, or had they to go one by one? I was afraid to ask the missionary to interpret such a question.

The advantage of being on a slow train was that there was time to see the country. In one vegetable garden, a man was using a plough, the like of which I had only hitherto seen in Bible pictures.

Once I thought I had a glimpse of a wedding, for people

were gathered in the yard of the house and there was much shouting and beating of drums and display of quantities of red colouring.

Here was a small boy seated on the back of a buffalo cow, either watching his father's flock of goats, or keeping away the crows from the rice crop; there, a huge sail appeared to be moving slowly across fields: where there is a sail moving it is safe to presume there is a boat and where there is a boat, it is equally safe to presume there is water, but all that could be seen was a sail in a field.

The Chinese live in villages and go out to their little patches of ground called by courtesy, farms. Even in the country everything looked dirty; the goats appearing to be the only clean things, and they may only have appeared clean because they were in the distance. Of course, I must acknowledge I was there in December, or winter weather.

At Neziang, the train waited one hour at the station, which was a mile from the village; gathered there were 250 people to see the foreigners and listen to what the missionary had to say. The latter was conversing on ordinary topics, endeavouring to make a good impression and thus pave the way for what was her particular duty. I noticed a man and woman asking her something earnestly and often, and afterwards learnt they were inviting the missionary to their home to talk to the people.

The two Chinese policemen in charge of the station had their numbers in both English and Chinese, as were also the names of all the stations.

This account is short but so was the journey—only ten miles.

As our trip came to an end, an old Chinese *amah,* who had travelled the world around several times, who had spent a year or more in Europe, and some months in America, was asked, "*Amah,* you have lived in Europe where you have seen the beautiful cities, and gardens fragrant with flowers, and buildings as beautiful as you can make; you have been in America, and have seen the wonderful things done there in a short time. Now, of all the places where you have been in which would you prefer to live?" The old servant thought for a long time, her thoughts accompanied by many doubtful headshakes. Of course the expected answer was China, for one would rather live in one's own country, but the answer that came after due consideration was, "Well, ah, well, eggs are cheapest in Peking."

Now, when we think of it, how like we are to this old Chinese *amah*. Good food—or rather food to our taste—is an important factor in making a place desirable to live in. I have heard people discussing a European trip and say "Venice? Ah, that was where the hotel menu was abominable: Rome? Do you remember the delicious meals there? Paris? You should taste the French cooking." Is not that familiar? How different, after all, are any of us?

In 1904 Alexander MacLean was
appointed Commercial Agent to
Japan, where he arrived with his
daughter Margaret in the midst
of the Russo-Japanese War. The
next year Margaret set out for
China. The China she saw was
very different from the China
of today. She writes of swarms
of filthy people shouting and
jostling one another, of rick-
shaws and wheelbarrows laden
with people and freight, of
prisoners tied by their pigtails,
of beggars with hideous sores.
She writes of being caught in
a riot in Shanghai where sixty
people were killed, barely
escaping with her life. And
she writes of the beauty of
China and its persistent mystery.
Chinese Ladies at Home, as she
called her account of the last
days of the Manchu Dynasty, was
printed in 1906 but soon went out
of print. Many years later it
was rediscovered and is now
available again in a modern
edition with vignettes
by Elizabeth Stapells.

ISBN 0 88750 805 7 HC
ISBN 0 88750 806 5 SC

Printed in Canada